THE EROTICS
OF RESTRAINT

ALSO BY DOUGLAS GLOVER

NOVELS

Precious
The South Will Rise at Noon
The Life and Times of Captain N
Elle

STORY COLLECTIONS

The Mad River
Dog Attempts to Drown Man in Saskatoon
A Guide to Animal Behaviour
16 Categories of Desire
Bad News of the Heart
Savage Love

NONFICTION

Notes Home from a Prodigal Son
The Enamoured Knight
Attack of the Copula Spiders

THE EROTICS OF RESTRAINT

ESSAYS ON LITERARY FORM

Douglas Glover

A JOHN METCALF BOOK

BIBLIOASIS
Windsor, Ontario

Library and Archives Canada Cataloguing in Publication

Glover, Douglas, 1948–, author
The erotics of restraint : essays on literary form / Douglas Glover.

Issued in print and electronic formats.
ISBN 978-1-77196-291-9 (softcover).—ISBN 978-1-77196-292-6 (ebook)

1. Literary form. 2. Authorship. I. Title.

PS8563.L64E76 2019   C814'.54   C2018-904456-X
C2018-904457-8

Edited by John Metcalf
Copy-edited by James Grainger
Text and cover designed by Gordon Robertson

Published with the generous assistance of the Canada Council for the Arts, which last year invested $153 million to bring the arts to Canadians throughout the country, and the financial support of the Government of Canada. Biblioasis also acknowledges the support of the Ontario Arts Council (OAC), an agency of the Government of Ontario, which last year funded 1,709 individual artists and 1,078 organizations in 204 communities across Ontario, for a total of $52.1 million, and the contribution of the Government of Ontario through the Ontario Book Publishing Tax Credit and Ontario Creates.

PRINTED AND BOUND IN CANADA

CONTENTS

THE STYLE OF ALICE MUNRO

So I felt obliged, out of contrariness. . . .
— from "Baptizing"

WE HAVE here to speak of style in a double sense: style as the basket of syntactic moves habitual to an author, but also style as tilt, the characteristic lean or bearing of the author as she represents herself through her writing. Call the latter personality, power, or panache. Alice Munro comes from a part of the world that challenges both eccentricity and ambition (and is not necessarily able to tell the two apart). "Who do you think you are?" the townspeople of her fictional southwestern Ontario town ask. As if in response to this challenge, Munro forges her style in the furnace of opposition. She plays with expectation and denial of expectation; she insists upon difference. My sense is that she doesn't compose so much by reference (to a notional reality) as by dramatic antithesis. A statement provokes a counterstatement or a counter-construct, subversion, or complication, and the sentences, paragraphs, and stories advance by the accumulation of such contraventions. The initial statement, the facticity of the story, then, by steps and countersteps, implicates itself in a series of deferrals that render it less unequivocal and more inflected as it progresses. The truth is never the truth but a truth with codicils, conditions, caveats, perorations, and contradictions.

For me the quintessential moment in the contrarian edifice of Alice Munro's oeuvre takes place in her story "Lives of Girls and Women" (in the book of the same name), when Del Jordan climbs into the car with Chamberlain expecting sex only to find herself enlisted to spy on her mother's boarder, the vegetal Fern. "I brought my mind back, slowly, from expectations of rape," writes Munro in the voice of Del. My liberal education has armoured me against such thoughts, anathematized men wanting to rape women and men who think that women want to be raped. But in "Lives of Girls and Women," Munro has written a character, somewhat like herself, who climbs into an older man's car wanting sex. The lovely word "slowly," the fulcrum of the sentence, indicates the trouble, the reluctance, involved in readjusting to the disappointment of the flesh. Del has already made herself available on a casual basis for illicit caresses, child molesting, in fact. She has admired the brutality of her erstwhile lover's slaps and pinches. When she thinks about "criminal sensuality," it is her own, not Chamberlain's.

What interests me is less the thematics of the case than the structural and syntactic aspect of Del's rape reveries, which are purely oppositional. They place her outside conventional cultural norms. She colludes with the bad man to bring about her own sexual degradation. Though in many ways Chamberlain is her notional antagonist, it would be disingenuous to say they are in conflict precisely. More significantly, in terms of the story's syntax, Del's fantasies place her in opposition to her mother. Mrs. Jordan is a modern woman of her time, an erstwhile provincial intellectual, a proto-feminist, cultured in a superficial, self-flattering way, slightly comical in the Dickens mode, with her encyclopedia business and her opera books. She creates herself in opposition to her husband (she has left the family house on Flats Road and moved into town with Del) and to the community of Jubilee, which, to her, is rural, ignorant, petit bourgeois, and philistine. It's enough for the town to be suspicious of someone for Mrs. Jordan's allegiance to lean in the opposite direction. She's also ambitious for her daughter, reads the university catalogues, and dreams of courses she would take if she were Del. She's puritanical about sex, despite her liberalism. So much so that when Jerry Storey's mother begins talking to her about diaphragms, Del finds herself offended and, briefly, prefers her mother's silence on sexual matters. But, crucially for Del, her mother is the anvil on which she hammers out her selfhood.

In the last paragraph of "Lives of Girls and Women," Del isn't thinking of the erotic debacle with Chamberlain; she is instead rejecting her mother's advice for young women, the whole earnest speech about the change coming in "the lives of girls and women," which incidentally ironizes the title of the book.

> I did not quite get the point of this, or if I did get the point I was set up to resist it. I would have had to resist anything she told me with such earnestness, with such stubborn hopefulness. Her concern about my life, which I needed and took for granted, I could not bear to have expressed. Also I felt that it was not so different from all the other advice handed out to women, to girls, advice that assumed being female made you damageable, that a certain amount of carefulness and solemn fuss and self-protection were called for, whereas men were supposed to be able to go out and take on all kinds of experiences and shuck off what they did not want and come back proud. Without even thinking about it, I decided to do the same.

Lives of Girls and Women, which was published as a novel, is a novel of sorts, a very loosely constructed novel based around a series of stories in the life of a character named Del Jordan in a town called Jubilee in southwestern Ontario. The stories progress chronologically through Del's girlhood (stories about neighbours, ancestors, older relatives, her mother, her early religious enthusiasm) to the summer after she graduates from high school. Each of the chapters functions more like a short story than a chapter. Aside from the progressive chronology and the fact that the some characters recur, there isn't a lot of novelistic development (motivational consistency, expanding symbols, tie-backs, and memory rehearsals typical of novels) from one story to the next. This structure alters in the second half of the book, in particular with the run of three stories: "Changes and Ceremonies," "Lives of Girls and Women," and "Baptizing," which all feature Del in an erotic (or romantic) relationship with a male character.

In "Changes and Ceremonies," Del's erotic attachment amounts to a crush on a boy, Frank Wales, who acts the Pied Piper in her school play, can't spell, and subsequently drops out of school and finds a delivery job for a dry cleaner. Del is only in Grade Seven, and her desire functions at the level of fantasy and girlish banter with her friend Naomi. In "Lives of Girls and Women," she is about fourteen—somewhere between Grade Seven and her "third year of high school," where she is when the next story, "Baptizing," begins. "Changes and Ceremonies" is a thematic and structural pre-story to the two long and blazing masterpieces—"Lives of Girls and Women" and "Baptizing"—that form the dramatic and thematic core of the book. The three-story sequence is more novel-like (with a consistent motivation throughout) in the conventional sense than the book as a whole, if it really matters what you call it.

"Lives of Girls and Women" is a thirty-page story that relates the details of Del's precocious involvement with Mr. Chamberlain, a local radio personality and a familiar presence at the Jordan house where he comes to visit the boarder, Fern. The story advances in a conventional style. In the fifth paragraph, Del states her desire: "It was glory I was after, walking the streets of Jubilee, like an exile or a spy. . ." Later in the story, glory is associated with sex, and later still, in "Baptizing," the link is made explicit when she connects the blood from her lost virginity with glory. "When I saw the blood the glory of the whole episode became clear to me." In the first plot step of the story, Chamberlain arouses Del by talking about the teenage prostitutes he had seen in Italy during the war. In the second plot step, she flirts with him in a gaminesque way and he touches her breast (after this she makes herself readily available to his caresses). In the third plot step, she gets into Chamberlain's car (expecting to be raped), but he surprises her by asking her to spy on Fern instead (he is afraid certain letters might implicate him in a breach-of-promise suit). And in the fourth plot step, she climbs into Chamberlain's car, they drive into the country, and he masturbates in front of her.

The structure of the story is elaborated. There is the mother who forms, as I say, an oppositional dipole with Del; also a side plot involving Chamberlain and the boarder Fern; and there is a subplot involving Del's friend Naomi and her family (Munro is always setting up these parallel contrasts: characters, families, ways of speaking, even homes and neighbourhoods). Naomi is similarly fascinated by sex, but she does not find an object of desire. While Del is running after Chamberlain, Naomi falls ill, and, when she revives, she is strangely reticent but exhibits a droll false consciousness in regard to sexual matters—this is enunciated in a sentence marvelous for its series of rhythmic deferrals.

> All the grosser aspects of sex had disappeared from her conversation and apparently from her mind although she talked a good deal about Dr. Wallis, and how he had

sponged her legs himself, and she had been quite help-lessly exposed to him, when she was sick.

"Baptizing" is a mirror story but the opposite (the way the left hand is related to the right hand), a story of consummated desire. It's very long, fifty-four pages, a novella really, and the action comes three years after "Lives of Girls and Women." The two stories form a diptych, a knowing juxtaposition. Naomi and Del are in high school, but Naomi quickly trans-fers to the commercial stream, then leaves school for a job in the creamery. What follows is a variation of conventional plot structure. Whereas in the previous story Del dealt only with Chamberlain, in "Baptizing" there are three large plot steps, each involving a different man: 1) Del goes to the Gay-la Dance Hall with Naomi and ends up drinking in a hotel room with Naomi, Naomi's boyfriend Bert Matthews, and a man named Clive. 2) Del has a hilarious if somewhat clinical sexual encounter with her high school intellectual peer Jerry Storey. (Both these encounters end ignominiously with Del escap-ing across town in the night on foot.) 3) She has a delicious, all-out love affair with a Baptist mill worker named Garnet French. We should note here that this strategy of varying plot structure by using different antagonists in each plot step is also used in James Joyce's "The Dead," in which the protago-nist Gabriel has dramatic interactions with three successive women, Lily, the maid, Miss Ivors, the fellow journalist, and, finally, his wife.

Each of these major plot events is stepped out, that is, each one is broken up into a series of steps, so that they form a min-iature story, a dramatic whole within the larger structure of the entire story. For example, the Gay-la Dance Hall sequence involves a setup (Naomi urging Del to accompany her), walk-ing to the dance hall, the entry between rows of men, danc-ing with Clive, buying drinks (Del is quite happy to drink the whiskey straight), driving to the hotel, hanging about in the hotel room, Del going down the corridor to the bathroom, Del letting herself down the fire escape, Del walking back to Naomi's house and waking her father, Del walking back to her own house and going to bed, and finally Naomi waking Del the next morning, debriefing and aftermath.

The first two plot events (Clive and Jerry Storey) are hilarious, almost slapstick. They are different events but quite parallel in structure. Both involve Del in a kind of dead-pan comic anarchy of desire (drunken Del hanging from the fire escape, clinical Del being bundled naked into the cellar as Jerry Storey's mother arrives through the front door). Both involve comically maladroit erstwhile lovers. Both climax in an escape and a walk home in the night. Here it's fascinating to track the parallels and contrasts between the darker flawed sexual attempt with the ineffable Chamberlain and the farcical escapades with Clive and Jerry. This is a standard Munro structure: inflect by juxtaposition and contrast.

The final plot event in "Baptizing," the Garnet French episode, is altogether different in that the sexual encounter proposed at the outset is successfully consummated (at night, in the side-garden against the wall of her mother's house). Del and Garnet have a wonderful sex life for the brief weeks that they are together, until the relationship collapses under the weight of internal contradictions that Del has been blissfully ignoring. Garnet wants her to be baptized, join his church (instead of just attending his youth group meetings), and get married, whereas Del has no interest in being subordinated to his mission. She has a secondary desire in the story, to win a scholarship and go to university. But that's not the reason she brings up in the final scene with Garnet, when he tries to force a symbolic baptism in the Wawanash River where they go swimming. What she actually thinks during this scene is highly instructive.

[My emphasis throughout.] "Say you'll do it then!" His dark, amiable but secretive face broken by rage, a helpless

> sense of insult. I was ashamed of this insult but had to
> cling to it, because it was only **my differences, my res-
> ervations, my life** ... I thought I was fighting for **my life**.

The words "differences" and "reservations" are crucial, also the
way they are identified with the girl's life, her very self. This
scene is a structural duplicate of the masturbation scene in
"Lives of Girls and Women." In both texts, Del has been playing an erotic game. Both scenes take place outside, in a locale
of rural privacy. But, typically for Munro, the scenes present
a contrast. Oddly enough, the sleazy encounter with Chamberlain, the semen on her skirt, does not threaten Del's sense
of self. She doesn't feel like a victim and doesn't want her
encounter to be categorized in a way that portrays her as a
victim. In "Baptizing" she's resisting Garnet, but in "Lives" she
is, in contrast, not resisting Chamberlain; instead she's resisting her mother (and her mother's proto-feminist notion of
female self-respect).

In "Baptizing," dramatic opposition between Del and
her mother still exists but in a slightly oblique way. The relationship with Garnet develops quickly in opposition to the
desire Del shares with her mother to get good grades and win
a scholarship to university. Del loses focus in a fog of erotic
bliss the day after she loses her virginity and can barely concentrate during an important examination. When the grades
come, her mother's dreams for her are finally defeated. But, as
in "Lives of Girls and Women," Del herself is not defeated or
dismayed or, in the least, self-critical; rather she is strength-
ened, more resolute and determined.

> Now at last without fantasies or self-deception, cut off
> from the mistakes and confusion of the past, grave and
> simple, carrying a small suitcase, getting on a bus, like
> girls in movies leaving home, convents, lovers, I sup-
> posed I would get started on my real life.

However, it does not escape the reader that, true to form, Del's final resolve is itself a theatrical (playful) construct of cinematic fantasy.

The stylistic lesson is that though Munro produces a facsimile of a conventional, naturalistic narrative (she pays her dues to verisimilitude, even going so far as to use "facts" from her own life to tease the reader) that moves forward in a series of plot steps in chronological order, there is another structure imposed on the narrative, a static structure of repetitions, mirrors, and contrasts. "Baptizing" repeats the theme and plot of Del's sexual desire from "Lives of Girls and Women," but with the difference that in "Baptizing" Del achieves the sexual glory denied her by Chamberlain. "Baptizing" also repeats the structure of resistance and separation (individuation) between Del and her mother. Both stories develop internal repetitions as well. In "Lives of Girls and Women," the second and third plot steps involve Del getting into Chamberlain's car (and being disappointed of her desire both times). In "Baptizing," the first and second plot events both involve comic erotic catastrophes and Del walking home across town in the dark.

This system of composing by parallel and antithesis extends to Munro's subplots. In a Munro narrative, rarely are characters invented alone (they will normally have a relational other) nor are they static in time; they have their own stories and plots. In both "Lives of Girls and Women" and "Baptizing," Naomi serves as a dipole for Del; she is friend, confidante, co-conspirator, and ally (apparently the same but different), and she has her own plot. In both stories, Del and Naomi start together at the Go square, then diverge. In "Lives of Girls and Women," they are twinned until the moment Del turns secretive about her interaction with Chamberlain. As Del pursues her affair with Chamberlain, her relationship with Naomi fades; Naomi goes underground herself, falling ill and remaining secluded at home except for visits from the doctor. When the two young women start communicating at the end of the story, they are in surprisingly different places: Naomi no longer wants to talk and joke explicitly about sex (though she will dwell on how the doctor washed her) and Del has achieved a dark and secret knowledge of sexuality that she is not willing to divulge.

In "Baptizing," the girls are co-conspirators in the Gay-la Dance Hall episode, but as in the previous story, they diverge. Naomi is disappointed in Del for making a mess of the hotel drinking scene, and Del isn't interested in repeating that sort of mischief. Naomi disappears from the story through the Jerry Storey episode. We don't know what's been happening to her until the primary plot of the story has nearly reached completion and Del is at the peak of her involvement with Garnet French. Then we learn Naomi's story retrospectively: a series of lovers, accidental pregnancy, projected marriage (without love). Del has been receiving warnings against the disastrous consequences of pregnancy throughout the story, a recurring motif, the steady drumbeat of pragmatic female concern. Yet she enjoys glorious sex and escapes unscathed, whereas Naomi's sexual history sounds like a chore, and she ends up trapped. Their two plots diverge but balance each other symmetrically as opposing outcomes.

Munro composes Jerry Storey as a subplot as well. He and Del are twinned as male and female star scholars with similar academic ambitions, though (and with Munro there is always a though or a but) Jerry's bent is toward the scientific whereas Del favours the humanities, and Jerry's attitude toward Del's intelligence is condescending and chauvinistic. It's worth mentioning that I think this is the only time in Munro's oeuvre that she mentions the Nobel Prize, and Jerry Storey is the one who contemplates winning it. This makes you wonder what Munro was thinking, all those years ago.

> After he said something like this he would always mutter, "You know I'm kidding." He meant about the Nobel Prize,

not the war. We could not get away from the Jubilee belief that there are great, supernatural dangers attached to boasting, or having high hopes of yourself. Yet what really drew and kept us together were these hopes, both denied and admitted, both ridiculed and respected in each other.

But after their opera bouffe erotic contretemps, their plots diverge as well. Del falls for Garnet French and her studies suffer. When last we hear of Jerry, he is sending Del post-cards from the road as he tours the American states with his mother, reading Marx in restaurants "TO ASTONISH THE NATIVES." In other words, starting from the same ground (teenage scholars living with their mothers), they end up in symmetrically opposed outcomes: Jerry paired with his mother and Del, ultimately alone and free ("I was free and I was not free" is what she thinks, continuing the pattern of inflection by antithesis), having separated from both her mother and Garnet French.

Such structural strategies are everywhere in Alice Munro's fiction. She is very good at concealing her art behind a screen of apparently naturalistic detail that, when read carefully, turns out to be a highly formal elaboration of finite elements.

In addition to the plot repetitions, Munro packs her texts with apparently tangential scenes made to cohere by the technique of thematic forcing. In "Lives of Girls and Women" the sexual theme is stamped everywhere. When Del visits Naomi's house and Naomi's father makes them read a passage from the Bible (Matthew 25, 1-13), Del thinks:

> I had always supposed this parable, which I did not like, had to do with prudence, preparedness, something like that. But I could see that Naomi's father believed it to be about **sex**.

Del and Naomi walk through town together (an off-plot inter-
lude), only to end up watching Pork Childs' peacocks. The four
paragraphs beginning "And the peacocks crying . . ." lead to a
repetition of that word "glory"—"Glory in the cold spring, a
wonder in Jubilee"—and end with Naomi's exclamation, "It's
sex makes them scream." In each of these scenes, something
non-sexual is stamped with the word sex; while in the same
story, Munro inserts the brothel paragraph (Del just ponder-
ing the brothel at the edge of town), in which something conventionally sexual is stamped with the domestic and ordinary
(the inverse). "One of them was reading the *Star Weekly*." And
when Del goes to search Fern's bedroom, she finds birth control information and pornographic doggerel. "(*A big cock in
my pussy is all it would take!*)" Of all the possible things Del
could have found, the author opts for the marker of sexuality.

In the same vein of structural repetition, in "Baptizing,"
as mentioned, there are three men—Clive, Jerry Storey, and
Garnet French—each in parallel situations with Del but clearly
contrasted in personality. Studious Jerry is the near opposite
of the shadow-boxing jokester Clive, and Garnet is the Baptist
mill worker opposite of nerdy Jerry Storey. (Note also the contrast between Clive and Garnet: Clive shadow-boxes to punc-
tuate his masculine banter, while Garnett went to jail for nearly
beating a man to death; Clive drinks, Garnet does not.) In many
cases, Munro supports the contrasts with commentary. We can
take the following to represent a typical Alice Munro sentence.

> It was **the very opposite** of going out with Jerry, and see-
> ing the world dense and complicated but appallingly
> unsecretive; the world I saw with Garnet was something
> not far from what I thought animals must see, the world
> without names.

But also notice the repetition of the dinner scenes: Jerry
and Garnet each come to dinner at Del's house; Del has din-

ner at Jerry's house and also at Garnet's house. Tellingly, the dinner sequence at Garnet's house is amplified and elaborated, a Dickensian, jolly, underclass sprawling family, a set-piece contrast to the other dinners in several ways. Just as in "Lives of Girls and Women" Naomi's household is contrasted with Del's, in "Baptizing," the Jordan, Storey and French households are framed together, an ironic triptych of multiple contrasts and parallels. For example, both Jerry and Del live alone with their mothers; both mothers are "modern" but in surprisingly different ways. By contrast the rural poverty of the French household is remarkably lively, tolerant, accepting, rambunctious and, well, healthy. Says Garnet's mother: "It looks pretty plain to anybody from town, but we always get enough to eat. The air's lovely, in summer anyway, lovely and cool down by the creek. Cool in the summer, protected in the winter. It's the best situated house I know of."

Munro carefully plans these dinner scenes right down to the food. At the Jordan house:

> I was critical of the meal, as I always was before company; the meat seemed underdone, the potatoes slightly hard, the canned beans too cool.

At Storey house:

> For dessert we had molded Jello pudding in three colours, rather like a mosque, full of canned fruit.

At the French house:

> For supper we had stewed chicken, not too tough, and good gravy to soften it, light dumplings, potatoes ("too bad it's not time for the new!"), flat, round, floury biscuits, home-canned beans and tomatoes, several kinds of pickles, and bowls of green onions and radishes and

leaf lettuce, in vinegar, a heavy molasses-flavoured cake,
blackberry preserves.

In this case, Del herself nails the moral of the contrast: "There
is no denying I was happy in that house."

Menu lists are not inherently dramatic, only become
dramatic within a system of contrasts wherein they acquire
meaning in excess of mere realistic description. These structural repetitions are a matter of style. Munro is not just telling a
story but creating a complex pattern of repetition and contrast
over and above the mere story. Although she is concerned with
what comes next, the chronological thread of narrative, she
clearly also composes with an eye to elaborating this system of
repetitions, parallels, reflectors, and contrasts. Munro deliberately juxtaposes similar or parallel scenes to add a dimension
of meaning not contained in the mere story. Similar things—
characters, scenes, locations, families—are contrasted, and
different things are stamped with unexpected similarity, creating a complex structure of inter-relation, cross-reference, and
identity not, perhaps, reducible to a single, simple theme.

This formal elaboration and pattern-making matches the
author's irony, her "complexity and play-acting," against the
conventional expectation of a garden variety well-made story.
The first lesson of any Munro story is that the story will resist
closure, will resist easy summations and quick definitions, it
will reach for complexity and irony over interpretation. Who
do you think you are? is exactly the question; and Alice Munro's answer is always, Not who you think I am. Not even who
you thought I was in the last sentence.

Resistance, complexity, and difference are the essential char-
acteristics of Munro's style. It should be clear by now that
many of the content choices Munro makes are based on a
structural demand for contrast. The demand for contrast, in

many cases, overrides or subverts the conventional demand for story efficiency. In "Lives of Girls and Women," there is no plot reason for the paragraph about the brothel; in "Baptizing," we don't need the dinner menus. These textual elements serve the story instead by creating an oscillating grid of similarity and difference. Similar structures are shown to be different; things that appear different at first are shown to be similar. This modus operandi extends from the macro or strategic level of form (the juxtaposition of plots, events, households, neighbourhoods, landscapes, social classes, genders, and character groups) to the micro level, the grammar of sentences and paragraphs, and thence outward again, to the level of character and theme, psychology and ethics.

Munro creates character by inventing contrast pairs; rarely does a person exist alone in a sentence, but instead finds complexity in a contrasting other, a dipole, either another character, or a subversion, or a denial of expectation. She doesn't say, X is Y; she says, X is different from Y, or X is Y but different in relation to Z. You can see this even at the level of sentences and paragraphs. Here, for example, is a description of Fern and Mrs. Jordan.

> All those qualities my mother had developed for her assault on life—sharpness, smartness, determination, selectiveness—seemed to have **their opposites** in Fern, with her diffuse complaints, lazy movements, indifferent agreeableness.

And here is a straight house-for-house contrast, Del and Naomi.

> Naomi was not popular in my house, nor I in hers. Each of us was suspected of carrying the seeds of contamination—in my case, of atheism, in Naomi's, of sexual preoccupation.

Household attitudes and moral culture are juxtaposed in two sentences using parallel construction.

Often Munro composes a sentence or a paragraph around a but-construction, using the word "but" or some cognate to create a dramatic shift in meaning. In "Lives of Girls and Women," Del's mother, Mrs. Jordan, and Fern listen to opera. Del's mother has a book about opera, but Fern once studied singing and is presumed to have inner knowledge.

> She had questions for Fern, **but** Fern did not know as much about operas as you would think she might; she would even get mixed up about which one it was they were listening to. **But** sometimes she would lean forward with her elbows on the table, not now relaxed, **but** alertly supported, and sing, scorning the foreign words.

The sentences zig-zag, turning at the buts, creating a complex and fundamentally sympathetic picture of Fern, a picture that accretes through a series of rhythmic deferrals until the last phrase. What is deferred is a final meaning as each "but" contradicts an assumption about Fern, replacing it with a new assumption, which is in turn contradicted.

There is a beautiful thematic passage in "Baptizing" that further illustrates Munro's use of this grammatical technique. It occurs when Garnet and Del are exploring their sexuality without yet having had intercourse, wild sessions of making out and petting in his parked truck or in the woods by the river. Note how Munro employs the not/but-construction to juxtapose contrasting ideas.

> I would go home from these sessions by the river and not be able to sleep sometimes till dawn, **not** because of unrelieved tension, **but** because I had to review, could not let go of, those great gifts I had received, gorgeous bonuses—

lips on the wrists, the inside of the elbow, the shoulders, the breasts, hands on the belly, the thighs, between the legs. Gifts. Various kisses, tongue touchings, suppliant and grateful noises. Audacity and revelation. The mouth closed frankly around the nipple seemed to make an avowal of innocence, defenselessness, **not** because it imitated a baby's **but** because it was not afraid of absurdity. Sex seemed to me all surrender—**not** the woman's to the man **but** the person's to the body, an act of pure faith, freedom in humility.

The three not/but-constructions create a stepped argument rising to that glorious and complex avowal of the nature of sex, all the more powerful because it is conscious of its opposite.

Sometimes the opposition will be inscribed in the diction. For example, Munro often uses the word "difference" to ascribe, yes, difference, to make a distinction. In the following extract, difference is registered subjectively (the difference frightens Del) as well as in the diction.

Well-groomed girls frightened me to death. I didn't like to even go near them, for fear I would be smelly. I felt there was a radical **difference**, between them and me, as if we were made of **different** substances.

Alice Munro stories are like assemblages of Venn diagrams, each circle defines a separate, autonomous, and different field (she uses the word "world" often to describe differential subjectivities). But there are areas of coincidence, where the circles overlap, and where people find a solidarity (always tentative and temporary), usually in opposition to someone or something else. It's almost impossible to parse a sentence like the following without the idea of a set of Venn diagrams in mind.

> Her agnosticism and sociability were often **in conflict** in
> Jubilee, where social and religious life were apt to be **one
> and the same**.

This sentence is constructed with the balanced antithesis of
an aphorism ("conflict" vs "one and the same"; "agnosticism
and sociability" v "social and religious life"), and part of the
reason for her compositional elegance is Munro's habit of
composing in opposed doubles. But the larger point is that
much of any Alice Munro text will be taken up with a precise
delineation of differences. Her style is to mark the differences.

The structural and syntactic vectors of difference, the various armatures of Munro's oppositional style, converge in the
character of Del Jordan, who is after all the one who is telling the story, the putative author. Sorting difference is Del's
way of experiencing the world and maintaining her sense
of self. It gives her a tilt, an attitude, a personality that is reso-
lutely and sometimes comically contrarian. In "Lives of Girls
and Women," she describes herself as "an exile or a spy"; in
"Baptizing," ". . . already I felt my old self—my old devious,
ironic, isolated self. . ." and "So I felt obliged, out of contrariness, to say. . ." At the sticking point in both stories, she finds
herself resisting the definitions of another character (I call
them definitions, but equally they could be called judgments
or behavioural expectations or forms): her mother's advice in
"Lives of Girls and Women"—"I did not quite get the point of
this, or if I did get the point I was set up to **resist** it. I would
have had to **resist** anything she told me with such earnestness,
with such stubborn hopefulness"—and Garnet French's mis-
sionary zeal in "Baptizing"—"and I felt amazement, not that I
was **fighting** with Garnet but that anybody could have made
such a mistake, to think he had real power over me."

Both stories express a universal plot, the drama of individuation, of the child separating from the mother; the mother is both literal and symbolic, acting as a placetaker for the matrix of supportive but ultimately limiting people and/or social structures that dog our lives. Both stories contrive to bring Del to a crisis of resistance, the point at which she encounters/discovers her self as a resisting presence as well as a clear sense of the difference between the other (the subjective world of the other) and the self she wishes to defend. Del asserts difference and selfhood without moralizing and without trying to create a type or archetype, asserting only individuality as a negative (I am not that) and, as a corollary, the mystery—inaccessibility—of the other. In other words, for Del, and for Munro, there are no essences, only what you might call subjective fields (family, friends, teachers, lovers, social groups), which have a tendency to impinge authoritatively (control, colonize) on the self.

But the fundamental difficulty with individuality (the irreducible difference of self) is in the encounter with another person and the paradoxical discovery that the self is a socially constructed artifact. In the cockpit of relationship, relating becomes an exchange of dimly perceived markers and signs, and the self becomes mysterious. Here is Del dancing with the Clive:

> "Dance me loose," he said, using one of these phrases, and rolling his eyes at me imploringly. I did not know what he meant; surely I was dancing with him, or he was dancing himself, as loose as anybody could do? Everything he said was like this; I heard the words but could not figure out the meaning; he might have been joking, but his face remained so steadily unsmiling. But he rolled his eyes this grotesque way, and called me "baby" in a cold languishing voice, as if I were someone altogether different

that the story text begins and ends at the same place. It begins with a present tense, italicized section of text that represents a notional now, then drops back in time to deliver the story setup, after which the narrative proceeds more or less chronologically. At the story's close, we return to the image introduced at the beginning.

The Stories

"The Point" is twenty pages long, divided into six sections by line breaks. Kurt Pittman, a thirteen-year-old boy, is the protagonist. His father, a medic in Vietnam, returned from the war with a Purple Heart but eventually shot himself. Kurt's mother is sad and drinks too much. They spend summers at a resort enclave on Puget Sound, across the water from Everett, Washington. Kurt's mother throws parties, and it's often Kurt's job to escort the inebriates home down the beach. The story opens with Mrs. Pittman getting Kurt out of bed to take Mrs. Gurney home. It's a windy night, the beach is in an uproar, and Mrs. Gurney is drunk and despairing because her husband doesn't love her any more.

Kurt's goal is to get her home; but Mrs. Gurney doesn't want to go home. What follows is a series of resistances: Mrs. Gurney sits down, wanders off, begins to shed clothes, talks (with unconscious cruelty) of killing herself, walks into the surf, and finally makes a sexual gesture in an attempt to seduce Kurt (the climax and testing point). Kurt struggles a moment with himself then pulls Mrs. Gurney together and walks her home.

That's technically the end of the plot, but, as I say, the text unrolls beyond that point into a lengthy story tail. Kurt retrieves one of his father's wartime letters from his bedroom and heads out to some swings along the beach to read it. The letter tells about the grotesque death of a soldier Kurt's father vainly tried to save. It also talks about despair. Then Kurt recalls his father's suicide, his discovery of his father's living but brain-dead body, and the terrible moments following when he runs back to tell his mother but cannot speak. This coda, this added material, is technically not story plot but backfill. Its placement at the end of the story is one of the author's delightful variations of conventional story structure.

The protagonist of "Shiloh"—a bit shorter in length than "The Point," broken up into seven sections—is a long-distance truck driver named Leroy Moffitt who's been injured in an accident and can no longer drive his rig. He and his wife Norma Jean live in a nondescript rented bungalow. Years before, when they were first married, they had a baby, but the child died of SIDS one night when they were at a drive-in movie, and the couple has existed on amiable but separate parallel tracks with Leroy spending long periods on the road. He vegetates at home now, smoking dope and building things from kits, which gives him the idea of building a log home for Norma Jean, a real home, he thinks, and a chance to reanimate their marriage. But Norma Jean doesn't want him to build a log cabin. Leroy persists without insisting.

Several plot scenes follow, in which the couple repeats versions of the same conflicted conversation. Leroy also replays the conflict meme when he buys marijuana from Stevie Hamilton, his dealer, telling Stevie he wants to build a log cabin but his wife doesn't want one. And he says much the same thing in a side scene with Mabel, Norma Jean's mother. Mabel serves a couple of structural functions in the story. She is Leroy's double in the sense that they both do crafts and they are both just passing time (example of doubling by homology). But Mabel is also a plot nudge, an accelerant. She goads Norma Jean to anger about her smoking and the dead baby, and she prods the couple to travel to the Shiloh battlefield, where Leroy finds his log cabin dream shot full of bullet holes. At the battlefield, Norma Jean tells Leroy she is leaving him.

Finally, "Brokeback Mountain" is the story of a pair of Wyoming cowboys, Ennis del Mar and Jack Twist, who meet one summer, herding sheep in the high pastures on Brokeback Mountain, where they become lovers. They are both nineteen at the outset. Their Edenic summer of love comes to an end with the August snow storms. Ennis goes back to working on failing cattle ranches, marries his sweetheart Alma Beers, and starts a family. Jack heads for Texas and brief career as a bull rider on the rodeo circuit. Four years later, Jack sends a postcard to Ennis, then drives north to Wyoming, and the two resume their love affair. Jack wants Ennis to buy a ranch with him, but Ennis is afraid of anything but the most closeted relationship. When he was a boy, his father had taken him to see the body of a murdered gay rancher.

The two men spend the next sixteen years meeting for so-called fishing trips, riding and camping through a series of mountain scenes, in hours stolen from work and family. Jack has married the daughter of a wealthy Texan; Ennis now has two daughters. Alma finally gets fed up with Ennis's secret sexual life (not secret from her) and leaves him for a more conventional and secure marriage with a grocer. The story climaxes on one of those mountain trips when Jack once again presses Ennis to come live with him, and Ennis demurs for the last time. The two never see each other again.

Jack is killed by an exploding tire, though Ennis remains convinced he was murdered. Ennis goes to Jack's family place, thinking he might convince the parents to let him take his friend's ashes to spread on Brokeback. But Jack's angry father won't let him. In a corner of Jack's bedroom closet, Ennis discovers a pair of shirts, one Jack's and the other his own, care-

Mrs. Gurney's resistance takes the form of action. Technically, the plot begins after the setup, as they leave the house—"Anyway, out the back door and down the steps." They struggle against the wind and blowing sand, but the first real plot resistance (just after the first line break) comes when Mrs. Gurney "plopped herself in the sand" and throws away her sandals. Kurt retrieves the sandals, stands her up, and gets her walking again; they reach the boardwalk where he commandeers a wooden wagon.

But then Kurt stops for a breather, and "Mrs. Gurney was gone." This is the second resistance event (plot step). He finds her back down the boardwalk in front of the Crutchfields' house (Crutchfield is a parallel story in the past, another drunk, another failed marriage, and another suicide, an example of homology in a subordinate storyline). Mrs. Gurney perches on an upturned boat and sheds her nylons. She gets to her feet, wanders toward the ocean, settles on a log, then vomits. All the while her spirits are worsening, self-pity and despair engulfing her heart. "I want to die," she says, after which she stumbles into the waves, trying to wash her skirt, then returns to the beach and lies down.

The third and climactic act of resistance begins after the fourth line break. Mrs. Gurney slumps to the sand again, shedding her blouse and brassiere. (Kurt keeps retrieving her cast off clothes.) There is some truth telling in this scene. Kurt says that he knows Mrs. Gurney's husband doesn't love her. Mrs. Gurney again says she'll kill herself. Kurt hands her her shirt, but the sea drags it from her shoulders, and her hand brushes the front of the boy's trunks. This is the crisis, the final moment of conflict; Mrs. Gurney's last act of resistance, of dragging Kurt away from his goal, is her drunken attempt at seduction. Kurt wavers in a thematically appropriate manner but comes firmly down on the side of duty and, offering Mrs. Gurney his T-shirt, escorts her the rest of the way home.

(Setup <small>father's suicide mentioned</small>) + **(Kurt/Mrs. G)**<small>Crutchfield backfill</small> +
(Kurt/Mrs. G)<small>Crutchfield again</small> + **(Kurt/Mrs.
G)**<small>Crutchfield again</small> + (Home) + (father's suicide
remembered)$^{time\ >>>}$

One device that often confuses the issue of plot for writing students is what I call "stepping out." Stepping out means dividing a single plot step into a series of smaller steps. This can give the impression of a welter of plot steps. For example, when Kurt and Mrs. Gurney leave the Pittman house, first they encounter the wind and blowing sand, then Mrs. Gurney plops down and throws off her sandals, then they converse, then Kurt gets her to her feet and they walk on, then he finds the wagon, etc. It's important not to be confused by this, but to essentialize such actions as a single step.

The full meaning of the story evolves from the interplay between several elements: Kurt's struggle to get Mrs. Gurney home, the Crutchfield backfill parallel story, the story of Kurt's father's time in Vietnam and his suicide, and a system of image patterns and thematic passages. But the concrete surface plot is very simple and clear (literally insisted upon by virtue of repetitive action and that home/goal meme). When you block out the plot text carefully, it's not difficult to see how the ancillary material fits between the plot events. And, as I say, the story text continues past the last plot step. Kurt returns to his own house, retrieves his father's letter, goes to the swings, reads the letter, and recalls finding his father still alive but dying from a gunshot to his head. This unconventional story tail is a capstone for the overall significance of the imagery, parallel backstory, thematic passages, and the suicide motif, and populates the subsurface moral level of the story, Kurt's own struggle with melancholy and despair.

Plot in "Shiloh"

In "Shiloh," Leroy Moffitt's plan to build his wife a log cabin provides the plot desire. He gets the idea from building a miniature log cabin out of Popsicle sticks (followed by a list of other artsy-craftsy projects). "At first the kits were diversions, something to kill time, but now he is thinking about building a full-scale log house from a kit." Norma Jean's response is a rejection. She says, "They won't let you build a log cabin in any of the new subdivisions." This is all within the first three paragraphs of the story and sets up the language (meme) of desire and resistance that repeats throughout. Leroy and Norma Jean keep getting together and raising the log cabin conflict (a story insists, it obsesses on its structure).

> "I'm aiming to build us a log house," says Leroy. "Soon as my plans come in."
> "Like *heck* you are," says Norma Jean.

> "I'm going to build you this house," says Leroy. "I want to build you a real home."
> "I don't want to live in any log cabin."
> "It's not a cabin. It's a house."
> "I don't care. It looks like a cabin."

> His mind has gone blank. Then he says, "I'll sell my rig and build us a house." That wasn't what he wanted to say. He wanted to know what she thought—what she *really* thought—about them.
> "Don't start on that again," says Norma Jean.

That's four scenes, four conversations, between Leroy and Norma Jean that iterate the conflict meme, which also recurs in two off-plot scenes. Off-plot scenes are satellite scenes with other characters, not the main conflict pair. Talking to Stevie Hamilton, his dealer, Leroy says,

> "I'm aiming to build me a log house, soon as I get time. My wife, though, I don't think she likes the idea."

Later, in a scene with Mabel, Norma Jean's mother, he reaffirms his realization.

> "I want to make her a beautiful home," Leroy says, indicating the Lincoln Logs. "I don't think she even wants it. Maybe she was happier with me gone."

I call this technique "forcing" because the author forces the conflict meme, like a signature or watermark, into parts of the story where it doesn't naturally belong. When Mason inserts a conflict meme in an off-plot scene she forces that scene to cohere within the structure of the story as a whole. This is evidence of an author's conscious control of her material. In "Shiloh," there are actually six scenes in which the conflict pattern repeats, yet they aren't all plot scenes.

But the way the plot carries the story in "Shiloh" is different from "The Point." The conflict remains at the level of almost casual conversation. These scenes aren't fights, not even squabbles (except between Mabel and Norma Jean), and the emotional intensity barely rises. Leroy realizes that Norma Jean doesn't want a log cabin. He smokes dope, does his craft projects, and dreams over his plans while Norma Jean does fitness exercises, takes a writing class, and plays the organ Leroy has given her. They even laugh together. Leroy's desire alone cannot push the story along, so Mason invents a nudge, a third character who provides the plot accelerant, in this case Mabel, who rides Norma Jean about her smoking and, waspishly, about the dead baby.

[Mabel] "Did you hear about the datsun dog that killed the baby?"

Norma Jean says, "The word is 'dachshund.'"

"They put the dog on trial. It chewed the baby's legs off. The mother was in the next room all the time." She raises her voice. "They thought it was neglect."

Though she's a third character, separate from the conflict pair, Mabel is carefully composed as psychological parallel to Leroy. They both do arts and crafts, and most significantly, they are both just passing time (homology). A passing-time text meme starts up on the opening page of the story in connection with kit projects. "At first the kits were diversions, something to kill time..." Later, Mabel drops by, Norma Jean is vacuuming, Leroy is looking at his blueprints. "'I'm just waiting for time to pass,' she [Mabel] says to Leroy drumming her fingers on the table." And a few paragraphs on, Norma Jean and Leroy are sitting together at the kitchen table. Leroy thinks, "Norma Jean is miles away. He knows he is going to lose her. Like Mabel, he is just waiting for the time to pass." This kind of association, insisted upon by the author, is crucial. Mason forces meaning and unity by creating her characters in tandem and by tagging them with a meme. Mabel and Leroy reciprocally implicate one another in the artsy-craftsy, dope-smoking pointlessness of their lives, and they both annoy Norma Jean, who has embarked upon a rigorous self-improvement regime.

The conflict text memes, obvious and repetitive, create the story's superstructure. Inside the aesthetic spaces created between the plot texts, there is backfill (mostly about the dead baby), off-plot scenes (with Stevie Hamilton and Mabel), imagery, memories, character thought, and thematic material. The climax of the plot is, of course, the appearance of a real log cabin, the historic log cabin at the Shiloh battlefield, shot full

of holes during the battle, an obvious visual joke on the nature
of Leroy's dreamy desires.

> Norma Jean passes the log cabin Mabel mentioned. It is
> surrounded by tourists looking for bullet holes.
>   "That's not the kind of log house I've got in mind,"
> says Leroy apologetically.
>   "I know *that*."

After which, Norma Jean announces that she is leaving Leroy.
Alone in the final scene, Leroy has a beautiful thematic passage about the mysteries of history and marriage, and the
story ends.

(Setup **cabin/no cabin**) + (backfill about baby's death) + (cabin/no cabin

drug dealer scene) + (more backfill about baby's death) + (**cabin/no**

cabin) + (**cabin/no cabin**) + (cabin/no cabin scene with Mabel) +

(**cabin/no cabin**) + (**battlefield cabin**) +

(thematic passage)time >>>

Plot in "Brokeback Mountain"

"Brokeback Mountain" is a love story, a romance, a tale of suffering for love. Ennis del Mar and Jack Twist love each other,
but there is a disproportion in their love. Jack wants to go the
limit and live with Ennis, but Ennis, scarred and scared by the
memory of a gay rancher beaten to death, refuses. That kernel
of resistance is the source of their suffering and the plot. The
story is long in terms of pages and in terms of chronology, but
it surges forward in three basic steps, each step stepped out
and delayed by a set of incremental subordinate actions.

    The text opens with the framing device (speaks to shape),
then drops back twenty years and delivers a conventional
setup—a description of the two cowboys, their upbringing,

and how they meet on the mountain the summer of 1963. Desire strikes one cold drunken night, like the lightning that crackles around the mountain (pathetic fallacy), neither boy expecting it, both denying they are gay but both equally enthusiastic. Yet the desire is mute and inexpressible outside of the opening situation. This is the first plot step but without a concrete resistance, save for the general aura of homophobia and the boys' naiveté.

One dialogue line foreshadows (by homology) the conflict to come. Ennis is supposed to tend camp and cook, while Jack is to sleep with the sheep in the pasturage, riding back and forth for meals. But Jack resents the arrangement. "Point is, we both should be in this camp." But Ennis goes along with what the boss wants, changes roles, and starts sleeping with the flock in Jack's place, until that fateful, drunken night when they start having sex. Then the August storms come, and they part for four years, time for the desire to achieve a critical mass and surface.

Four years later, Jack drives to Wyoming on a mission. Here is the plot conflict meme in dialogue (as we saw it in "Shiloh"):

> **"Friend," said Jack. "We got us a fuckin situation here. Got a figure out what to do."**
> **"I doubt there's nothin now we can do," said Ennis.** "What I'm sayin, Jack, I built a life up in them years. Love my little girls. Alma? It ain't her fault. You got your baby and wife, that place in Texas. You and me can't hardly be decent together if what happened back there"—he jerked his head in the direction of the apartment—"grabs on us like that. **We do that in the wrong place and we'll be dead. There's no reins on this one. It scares the piss out of me."**

And here it is again, repeated in the same scene.

[Jack] "Listen. **I'm thinkin, tell you what, if you and me had a little ranch together,** a little cow and a half operation, your horses, it'd be a sweet life…"

[Ennis] "Whoa, whoa, whoa. **It ain't going to be that way. We can't.** I'm stuck with what I got, caught in my own loop. Can't get out of it. Jack, I don't want to be like them guys you see around sometimes. **And I don't want to be dead.**"

After sixteen years of fishing trips in the western mountains, they confront their "situation" once more. With the passage of years, the terms have changed slightly. There is no talk of getting a ranch together; Ennis put an end to that dream long before. But it has become increasingly difficult for Ennis to get away for their periodic fishing trips.

"You know, friend, **this is a goddamn bitch of a unsatisfactory situation. You used to come away easy. It's like seein the pope now.**"

"Jack, I got a work. Them earlier days I used to quit the jobs. You got a wife with money, a good job. You forget how it is bein broke all the time. You ever hear of child support? I been payin out for years and got more to go. Let me tell you, **I can't quit this one. And I can't get the time off… You got a better idea?**"

"**I did once.**" The tone was bitter and accusatory.

A few lines down, Jack recapitulates the conflict meme, though now it is couched in the past, retrospectively, as a missed possibility.

"Try this one," said Jack, "and *I'll* say it just one time. Tell you what, **we could a had a good life together, a fuckin real good life. You wouldn't do it, Ennis.**"

Each of these plot steps, focused into a few lines of dialogue, is stepped out into a lengthy series of sub-events. For example, in the Brokeback Mountain sequence, the boys are hired on, go for beers, ride up into the mountains with the sheep, change roles, finally have sex, ignore the sheep, lose a lot of sheep, etc. As the story progresses, the filled-in material also includes a summary of Ennis's dysfunctional marriage to Alma Beers, their children, the divorce, a dinner party with her new husband and the kids, his slow economic decline. The story of Jack's marriage comes through dialogue. Soon after that last encounter by the Hail Strew River, Jack dies. This is aftermath; it follows the end of the plot. Ennis talks to Jack's wife on the phone, travels to see Jack's parents, fails to retrieve the ashes, and finds those shirts. It's important to note that even these sub-stories are plotted, stepped out, with their own conflict lines, not to be confused with the main conflict line, which forms the plot.

_(shirts & postcard) + **(1963 cowboys on Brokeback)** + (Ennis marries Alma) + **(1967 live together/not)** + (Ennis and Alma divorce) + **(1983 live together/not retrospectively)** + (Jack's death and aftermath) + _(shirts & postcard) time>>>

The key lesson is that stories have a plot, call it a surface plot if you wish to distinguish it from the larger meaning of the story. The plot is concrete, it evolves from a desire meeting a resistance. Desire meets resistance over and over in more intense and complex ways until they reach a climax. Authors do not veil plots or hint at them. In the stories under discussion, the plot elements (desire and resistance) are announced explicitly and repeatedly as text memes. Not only are the same actions repeated, they are often expressed in the same words.

Image Patterns, by Eros Claimed

The symbolic structure of a story rests on two foundations: the surface plot conflict and accumulated additional meaning supplied through image patterns, thematic passages, and backfill attached thereto. In "The Point," the plot conflict—Kurt wants to take Mrs. Gurney home but Mrs. Gurney doesn't want to go home—acquires a larger meaning in terms of stoicism and despair. In "Shiloh," the conflict—Leroy's desire to build Norma Jean a log cabin and her rejection of same—accrues a deeper meaning in terms of marriage, home, denial, and a couple's ability to repair the loss of their child. And in "Brokeback Mountain," Ennis's refusal to live with Jack connects with larger issues of closeting, homosexual fear, and endemic homophobia.

Image patterns are repetitive structures in the text. They are rhythmic and combinatory, the acme of the erotic, grounded in the wedding of word to word to create new meaning. Most commonly an image is some material thing available to sensory apprehension. The author begins to manipulate the image by simple repetition, then by loading it with specific associations. There are several loading techniques. The author can attach a piece of significant back story or a thematic passage to the image. The significant back story is significant because it will meaningfully attach the image to one of the principle characters or the plot conflict. The thematic passage will attach a general moral principle or philosophical stance to the image. The author can also construct meaning by association and juxtaposition, the methods of poetry. The author associates the image with some precisely focused descriptors using grammatical links such as "like" and "just as" or by parallelism or simply by writing them next to each other in the text.

The author can add complexity and elaboration by then splitting off associated elements into subsidiary or branch patterns (new lines of repetition), so that the root pattern unfurls tentacles into all parts of the text, extending and forcing the meaning and creating an organic unity. In some highly achieved image patterns, the author will practice a technique called tying-in, the device by which two or three (or even more) branch patterns are brought back together in the same sentence.

The Techniques of Image Patterning

1. Repetition
2. Loading
    a) Significant back story
    b) Thematic passages
    c) Association and juxtaposition
3. Splitting or branching
4. Tying in

Image patterning is both a device of artful elaboration and of authorial control. It boils down to a matter of simple repetition (plus splintering and the repetition of the branch patterns as well) that stamps the image (like a watermark) throughout the text. A useful exercise for readers is to locate all the tags, epithets, reflections, and descriptors associated with the image and list them in a notebook. This will give a neat summary of all the thoughts the author wanted the reader to think every time the image is mentioned. This obviates the need for speculative interpretation; most authors actually tell you their message. Certain critical theories about the death of the author and the primacy of reader response over authorial intention tend to discount how much conscious control an author exercises in literary fiction.

Image Patterns in "The Point"

Charles D'Ambrosio's "The Point" is a riot of patterning; he's a bit of a genius at patterning. "Black hole" is the root image.

You know this not because the words are repeated so often—they're not, only five times—but because the author attaches a thematic passage to the phrase and because it forms the central node of an expansive branching system. Black holes aren't even mentioned until seven pages into the story.

> It was that night, the night I took Mr. Crutchfield home, as I walked back to our house, that I developed **the theory of the black hole**, and it helped me immeasurably in this business of steering drunks around the Point. The idea was this—that at a certain age, a **black hole** emerged in the middle of your life, and everything got sucked into it, and you knew, forever afterward, that it was there, this dense negative space, and yet you went on, you struggled, you made your money, you had some babies, you got wasted, and you pretended it wasn't there and never looked directly at it, if you could manage the trick. I imagined that this **black hole** existed somewhere just behind you and also somewhere just in front of you, so that you were always leaving it behind and entering it at the same time. I hadn't worked out the spatial thing too carefully, but that's what I imagined. Sometimes **the hole** was only a pinprick in the mind, often it was vast, frequently it fluctuated, beating like a heart, but it was always there, and when you got drunk, thinking to escape, you only noticed it more. Anyway, when I discovered this, much like an astronomer gazing out at the universe, I thought I had the key—and it became a policy with me never to let one of my drunks think too much and fall backward or forward into the **black hole**. We're going home, I would say to them—we're just going home.

This kind of explicit thematic statement is essential to establishing story meaning and welding it to story action to make it symbolic. Kurt's theory of the black hole explains despair using an image and ties it unambiguously to the plot conflict: ". . . it became a policy with me never to let one of my drunks think too much and fall backward or forward into the black hole. We're going home, I would say to them— we're just going home." Getting Mrs. Gurney home becomes more than just walking her down the beach; Kurt is nudging her away from despair, offering her, if only momentarily, the option of following a stoic mode of conduct in the face of cruel existence.

But then you start to explore the wondrous branch lines, beginning with the word "black." "Black" leads to "dark" and "night" and "shadow" and "silhouette" and "Hat Island." "Dark" and "silhouette" appear in the first paragraph of the story (Kurt's tipsy mother appears first as "a looming silhouette"). Mrs. Gurney has a

> **dark tan**—the sort of **tan** that women around here get when their marriages start busting up. I could see the gaudy gold chains looped around Mrs. Gurney's **dark-brown** neck winking in the half-light before they plunged from sight into **the darker gulf** between her breasts.

The sky is "blue-black," the sea is "black," and far off, Kurt can see the "dark headlands of Hat Island."

> The **night** was sharp and alive with **shadows**—everything, even the tiny tufted weeds that sprouted through the sand, had **a shadow**—and this deepened the world, made it seem thicker, with layers, and more layers, and then a **darkness into which I couldn't see**.

All this precedes the "theory of the black hole" thematic passage quoted above, and just following it, Mrs. Gurney sheds her nylons "tossing the **little black doughnuts** into the wind." And a page later—this gorgeous, chilling sentence:

> Mrs. Gurney stared out across the water, at the **deep,**
> **black shadow of Hat Island**, and I looked, too, and it was
> remarkable, the way the **darkness carved itself out of**
> **the darkness all around**.

This is a good example of a tie-in line, pulling together the
darkness, black, and Hat Island branch patterns already running through the text.

During the climactic attempted seduction, Kurt describes
Mrs. Gurney's eyes as "glassy and dark and expressionless." The
dark of her neck, the gold jewelry, and the tan references return.

> The **nipples were purple** in the moonlight, and they
> puckered in the cold wind. The gold, squiggling loops of
> chain shone against the **dark of her neck**, and the **V of**
> **her tan** line...

The mascara starts running beneath Mrs. Gurney's eyes the
moment she touches his crotch—"two black lines pouring out
of them and running in crazy patterns down her cheeks." Out
on the swings, carrying his father's letter after delivering Mrs.
Gurney to her house, Kurt recalls the moment: "I thought of
Mrs. Gurney and her blank eyes and the black pouring out of
them." The effect, if you read solely for the image pattern, is
a surreal, perhaps hysterical, vision of the blackness of Mrs.
Gurney's despair (reflecting Kurt's own despair) liquefying,
gushing out of her, flooding the world.

Good stories are notable for their density of internal reference, their recursiveness and rhyme. I can only suggest
the full complexity of D'Ambrosio's story. There is a secondary word pattern of military language to remind us that the
father's career as a medic in Vietnam also colours the story.
Words like: hard-core veteran, mission, and the Vietnamese
slang *dinky dow* for crazy, *boom-boom*, etc. This is an important element of the story's moral construct, making a paral-

lel between the thirteen-year-old guiding drunks down the beach and his father rescuing soldiers during the war (action homology). There is also a pattern of nautical language that befits the coastal resort setting.

But most mysteriously, we likewise find an extended, painterly, purely aesthetic pattern of whiteness running through the text. This pattern works, so far as I can tell, simply by the logic of inversion and contrast. It has no added moral meaning except as a reminder of the black hole pattern.

> I looked up at the sky, and it was **black**, with some light. There were stars, millions of them like tiny **holes** in something, and the moon, like a bigger **hole** in the same thing. **White holes**.

> The moon was immaculately **white** in a **blue-black** sky.

> ... the **dark** of her neck, and the V of her tan line [earlier described as the "**darker** gulf"] made everything else seem astonishingly **white**.

> She looked out the window—at the **sail-white** moon beyond the **black** branches of the apple tree.

> Off to starboard, the sea was **black**, with a line of **moonlit white** waves continually crashing on the shore. Far off, I could see the **dark** headlands of **Hat Island**.

There is more of this, intricate and pervasive. I can, as I say, only suggest. I haven't even mentioned the silver pattern.

Image Patterns in "Shiloh"

Log cabins are the primary image pattern in "Shiloh," tipped in the title, which is a reference to that last scene when Leroy finally achieves the log cabin he has sought through the story, though it is not the log cabin of his dreams. The phrase "log cabin" repeats throughout due in part to its being Leroy's plot goal, but the phrase is also loaded precisely with meaning and occasions a lovely thematic passage at the story's close. This passage begins with a memory rehearsal, Leroy's summary of the story events, paralleling the history of the battle, then segues into a meditation on history, marriage, and the emptiness of his log cabin project.

> General Grant, drunk and furious, shoved the Southerners back to Corinth, where Mabel and Jet Beasley were married years later, when Mabel was still thin and good-looking. The next day, Mabel and Jet visited the battleground, and then Norma Jean was born, and then she married Leroy and they had a baby, which they lost, and now Leroy and Norma Jean are here at the same battleground. Leroy knows he is leaving out a lot. He is leaving out the insides of history. History was always just names and dates to him. It occurs to him that building a **house out of logs** is similarly empty—too simple. And the **real inner workings of a marriage, like most of history, have escaped him.** Now he sees that building **a log house** is the dumbest idea he could have had. It was clumsy of him to think Norma Jean would want **a log house**. It was a crazy idea.

The log cabin pattern originates in the story setup on the first page. Leroy is idle at home; he starts building things.

> He is not sure what to do next. In the meantime, he makes things from craft kits. He started by building a miniature log cabin from notched Popsicle sticks. He varnished it and placed it on the TV set, where it remains. It reminds him of a rustic Nativity scene.

Note the triviality inscribed in the Popsicle stick reference and the TV pedestal. But also notice the lorn loading established in the line about the Nativity scene. "It reminds him..." is a standard loading text establishing an association. A Nativity scene includes Mary, Joseph, and Jesus, mother, father, and son. The reader doesn't realize at first that the reference is heavy with absence and Leroy's own denial. The payoff arrives a few lines later with the background material about the death of Randy, Leroy's infant son, years before.

> They had a child who died as an infant, years ago. They never speak about their memories of Randy, which have almost faded, but now that Leroy is home all the time, they sometimes feel awkward around each other, and Leroy wonders if one of them should mention the child. He has the feeling that they are waking up out of a dream together—that they must create a new marriage, start afresh. They are lucky they are still married. Leroy has read that for most people losing a child destroys the marriage— or else he heard this on *Donahue*.

These lines on marriage explain Leroy's motivation going forward and reverberate later with the final thematic passage already quoted, on history, marriage, and log cabins. But at the outset they network the Popsicle stick cabin with Leroy's consciousness of his empty marriage and his intention to reanimate it by building a real home for Norma Jean. The disproportion between a Popsicle stick cabin and a rustic Nativity scene, between a kit and a real home and family, is intentionally ironic. It's part of the image pattern loading. In effect, Leroy writes his hopeful intentions into the image at the same time as Bobbie Ann Mason disperses hope with subversive references and irony. The point-of-view character tells one story while the image pattern tells another. The sentence about marriages destroyed by the loss of a child invokes the subtext, Leroy's marriage is already over.

Still on the first page, following the Nativity scene reference, Mason starts splintering her log cabin pattern. Rustic Nativity scene leads to "real home" (home is repeated) and thence to marriage and the absent baby. But the Popsicle stick log cabin also spawns a line of craft projects.

> Then he tried string art (sailing ships on black velvet), a macramé owl kit, a snap-together B-17 Flying Fortress, and a lamp made out of a model truck, with a light fixture screwed in the top of the cab. At first the kits were diversions, something to kill time but now he is thinking about building a full-scale log house from a kit.

This initial flare leads to a number of other, equally ineffectual activities. Each new activity is an element in the split-off branch pattern. The text associated with items on the branch line adds to the accumulated loading. Each package, so to speak, includes a critical shading, either the author's deadpan irony or a character's derision (Mabel or Norma Jean).

> "What's that thing?" Mabel says to Leroy in a loud voice, pointing to **a tangle of yarn on a piece of canvas**.
>
> Leroy holds it up for Mabel to see. **"It's my needlepoint,"** **he explains. "This is a** *Star Trek* **pillow cover."**
>
> **"That's what a woman would do,"** says Mabel. "Great day in the morning!"
>
> "All the big football players on TV do it," he says.
>
> "Why, Leroy, you're always trying to fool me. I don't believe you for one minute. **You don't know what to do with yourself—that's the whole trouble. Sewing!"**

The next day, Mabel drops by. It is Saturday and Norma Jean is cleaning. Leroy is studying **the plans of his log**

house, which have finally come in the mail. He has them spread out on the table—**big sheets of stiff blue paper, with diagrams and numbers printed in white**. While Norma Jean runs the vacuum, Mabel drinks coffee. **She sets her coffee cup on a blueprint.**

She [Norma Jean] sits at the kitchen table, **concentrating on her outlines [essay outlines for school]**, while Leroy **plays with his log house plans, practicing with a set of Lincoln Logs**.

"I want to make her **this beautiful home**," Leroy says, **indicating the Lincoln Logs**. "I don't think she even wants it. Maybe she was happier with me gone."

[Mabel] "She don't know what to make of you, coming home like this."

"Is that it?"

Mabel takes the roof off his Lincoln Log cabin. "You couldn't get me in a log cabin," she says. "I was raised in one. It's no picnic, let me tell you."

Mabel, as I say, is the plot nudge, but she's also linked psychologically and thematically with Leroy via the image pattern—she has her own inane fetish for empty activity; she keeps making dust ruffles.

Mabel is a short, overweight woman whose tight, brown-dyed curls look more like a wig than the actual wig she sometimes wears. Today she has brought Norma Jean **an off-white dust ruffle** she made for the bed; Mabel works in a custom-upholstery shop.

"This is the tenth one I made this year," Mabel says. "I got started and couldn't stop."

"It's real pretty," says Norma Jean.

"Now we can hide things under the bed," says Leroy,

who gets along with his mother-in-law primarily by jok-
ing with her.

In that first-page setup text, Leroy thinks of his little projects as diversions, "something to kill time." Later on, after resting her coffee cup on his house plans, Mabel says, "I'm just
waiting for time to pass." And another page later, Leroy thinks,
"Like Mabel, he is just waiting for time to pass." Using the
preposition "like" to link two characters with common traits
is standard procedure in story writing. But the link is mul-
tiply determined by homology (parallel actions) and by the
killing-time meme. Linking characters promotes coherence
and narrative economy as well as that density of internal reference I keep mentioning. But you begin to get an idea of how
dense and multifarious such linkages can be.

In this case, the reader really needs to understand this
connection, along with the image pattern branches, to appreciate the full effect of the story's accumulating resonances
tipped in the final sentence.

The sky is unusually pale—the color of the **dust ruffle
Mabel made for their bed**.

The last words of the story reference a subordinate branch
of the main image pattern, under the sign of vacuous projects, waiting for time to pass and sweeping things under the
bed. In fact, much of the action of this story takes place at
the level of image patterning, since the plot remains relatively
static, a repetition of positions. Leroy keeps saying he wants a
log cabin until finally he gets one shot full of holes. And then,
having been told his marriage is over, he admits the log cabin
was a crazy idea and that he doesn't understand marriage.
And the story ends by drawing the dust ruffle of silence over
the proceedings.

Image Patterning in "Brokeback Mountain"

The primary image pattern in "Brokeback Mountain" is, of course, Brokeback Mountain. The first reference is in the title. The second is in the italicized frame material at the beginning. First, indirectly: the two shirts shudder in a draft, but by the end of the story, we know that tacked above the shirts is a postcard view of Brokeback Mountain. Then, directly: Ennis recalling "that old, cold time on the mountain when they owned the world and nothing seemed wrong." This is the first meaning loaded into the image and it is retrospective; already composed as a symbol of a blissful, Edenic moment in the past.

Descriptions (loading) of the mountain through the first act of the story, the sheep herding sequence in 1963, are romantically turbulent.

> They found a bar and drank beer through the afternoon, Jack telling Ennis about **a lightning storm on the mountain** the year before that killed forty-two sheep, the peculiar stink of them and the way they bloated, the need for plenty of whiskey up there. **He had shot an eagle,** he said, turned his head to show **the tail feather in his hatband.**

Proulx frames images of the cowboys against the bulk of the mountain, fusing the image of the mountain with the image of the man.

> Dawn came glassy and orange, stained from below by a gelatinous band of green. **The sooty bulk of the mountain paled slowly until it was the same color as the smoke from Ennis's breakfast fire.**

> During the day Ennis looked across a great gulf and sometimes saw Jack, a small dot moving across a high

What Jack remembered and craved in a way he could neither help nor understand was the time that distant summer on Brokeback when Ennis had come up behind him and pulled him close, the silent embrace satisfying some shared and sexless hunger. . . Later, that dozy embrace solidified in his memory as **the single moment of artless, charmed happiness in their separate and difficult lives**.

In the aftermath (the surface plot is complete with Jack's death), Ennis telephones Jack's wife. Proulx loads the image pattern in dialogue, from an observer's point of view. Brokeback Mountain, as far as Lureen is concerned, was Jack's "place," possibly imaginary, a place where he might go to get drunk, but also the place where he wanted his ashes spread. This sends Ennis off on a supplementary quest, to respect Jack's last wish. Jack's father won't let him take the ashes, but Ennis finds those shirts. Here is how Proulx welds the shirts into the Brokeback image pattern:

He pressed his face into the fabric and breathed in slowly through his mouth and nose, hoping for the faintest smoke and mountain sage and salty sweet stink of Jack but there was no real scent, only the memory of it, **the imagined power of Brokeback Mountain of which nothing was left but what he held in his hands**.

Ennis proceeds to construct his little shrine to the mountain and to love. He buys a postcard—"scene a [sic] Brokeback Mountain."

When it came—thirty cents—he pinned it up in his trailer, brass-headed tack in each corner. Below it he drove a nail and on the nail he hung the wire hanger and the two old shirts suspended from it. He stepped back and looked at the ensemble through a few stinging tears.

Which brings us back to the shirts wafted by drafts in the italicized story opening.

I give all these quotations at length because this is the only way for the reader to appreciate how an author uses image patterning, loading, and branching to add and control meaning in a text. Only when you break out all the repetitions and loading texts can you begin to imagine what would be left if you took them out, how thin the story would be. Nor have I exhausted the patterning in Proulx's story. For example, you can walk back the story of the two shirts through the text via the repeated references to a punch Ennis delivered against Jack's jaw back when they were getting ready to leave the mountain in the first act. The dried blood on one of the shirt sleeves is a vestige of that blow. And there is a strong but separate "tire iron" pattern that originates in Ennis's memory of the old gay rancher Earl, beaten to death with a tire iron, possibly by Ennis's father. Later, Ennis suspects that Jack was beaten to death with a tire iron, and after talking to Jack's father, he's convinced of it.

The story closes, like "Shiloh," with a reference to a subsidiary image pattern, the tire iron, but with a fascinating little flourish. It's contained in one of Ennis's dreams, a reminder of the rich possibilities in dreams for creating surreal but telling linkages in a text.

> Around that time Jack began to appear in his dreams. Jack as he had first seen him, curly-headed and smiling and bucktoothed ... but the can of beans with **the spoon handle** jutting out and balanced on the log was there as well, in a cartoon shape and lurid colors that gave the dreams a flavor of comic obscenity. **The spoon handle was the kind that could be used as a tire iron.** And he

would wake up sometimes in grief, sometimes with the old sense of joy and release…

The Dali-esque morphing spoon is riveting, but you have to rifle the pages to find it again. Like Jack's eagle feather, the spoon and the can of beans only appear twice in the text. The first time is just before Jack's arrival from Texas at the beginning of the second act. Alma and Ennis are eating out at a restaurant, Ennis alert with anticipation.

> Alma was saying something about taking his friend to the Knife & Fork for supper instead of cooking it was so hot, if they could get a baby-sitter, but Ennis said more likely he'd just go out with Jack and get drunk. Jack was not a restaurant type, he said, thinking of **the dirty spoons sticking out of the cans of cold beans balanced on the log**.

The image meme links Jack to the memory of Jack's housekeeping skills, more precisely the spoons link to that time on Brokeback. The spoon and the tire iron remain separate image patterns until the final paragraphs of the story, where they are finally bolted together in the dream image. Spoons can transform into tire irons, which are the sign of the father law, homophobic rage, and violent death—the story's image ending hits the note of paradoxical impossibility, grief and joy alternating. The endings of "Shiloh" and "Brokeback Mountain" model a rule of thumb: image patterns can often provide elegant, inclusive, and poetic closure for a short story.

Thematic Passages, Mapping the Journey

A thematic passage is a text in which the author spells out the generalized meaning of the story, guiding the reader's interpretation of the action, giving it a moral and intellectual torque. Thematic passages express the soul of the story, they map its psychic territory. Any large statement containing the words "life" or "love" is likely to be a thematic passage. Thematic passages are the textual moments where the surface plot transcends local conditions and achieves universality or myth. They can be expressed by the narrator, in character thought, or even in dialogue.

You often find a lengthy thematic passage at the end of a story. But they also occur after a significant scene, or at the end of a subsection of text (a chapter, line-break section, for example). Sometimes they are attached to an image pattern or in the commentary between a plot and a subplot. Authors often use rhetorical questions to segue into a thematic passage. Climactic thoughts are sometimes couched as aphorisms. They show up any time the author needs to clarify the meaning of the action for the reader.

Crucially, thematic passages express the characters' own puzzlement over the situation they are in. At the very least, they open up obvious questions about the knot of trouble indicated in the plot conflict. These are questions that if not addressed, or at least raised, make the text (and characters) seem stultifyingly myopic and shut down. These are also the moments that give characters the impulse to new action.

Thematic Passages in "The Point"

In "The Point," the story of a thirteen-year-old boy leading a drunk woman home down the beach becomes the story of a thirteen-year-old boy battling private despair and grief (the memory and promise of suicide all around), who resists sexual temptation and finds the courage to proceed stoically and honourably with his mission. Kurt Pittman is an unusually self-conscious narrator; the story is packed with thematic material. I have already quoted the most extensive thematic passage, the text dealing with Kurt's theory of the black hole. But, just to be clear, here it is again:

> It was that night, the night I took Mr. Crutchfield home, as I walked back to our house, that I developed the theory of the black holes, and it helped me immeasurably in this business of steering drunks around the Point. The idea was this—that at a certain age, a black hole emerged in the middle of your life, and everything got sucked into it, and you knew, forever afterward, that it was there, this dense negative space, and yet you went on, you struggled, you made your money, you had some babies, you got wasted, and you pretended it wasn't there and never looked directly at it, if you could manage the trick. I imagined that this black hole existed somewhere just behind you and also somewhere just in front of you, so that you were always leaving it behind and entering it at the same time. I hadn't worked out the spatial thing too carefully, but that's what I imagined. Sometimes the hole was only a pinprick in the mind, often it was vast, frequently it fluctuated, beating like a heart, but it was always there, and when you got drunk, thinking to escape, you only noticed it more. Anyway, when I discovered this, much like an astronomer gazing out at the universe, I thought I had the key—and it became a policy with me never to let one of my drunks think too much and fall backward or forward into the black hole. We're going home, I would say to them—we're just going home.

Basically, this is a little essay that outlines a theory of life that Kurt has evolved watching adults as he conducts them on their drunken journeys along the beach. The black hole is despair, anomie, depression—call it what you will. The word "depression" shows up in the story in a sentence that links, by parallelism (that sense of being poised or balanced between a hole in front and a hole behind), with the theory of the black hole passage.

> Often my drunks seemed on the verge of sobering up, and then, just as soon as they get themselves **nicely balanced**, they plunged off the other side, into **depression**.

This black hole passage combines theory and practice; D'Ambrosio is careful to connect black holes with Kurt's motivation, his modus operandi in dealing with his drunks. Kurt's flat insistence on getting Mrs. Gurney home is a matter of policy that also hooks up with a parallel text in Kurt's father's letter from Vietnam (thus completing a pairing of father and son implicit in Kurt's memory, the Vietnam-era diction, and the fact that Kurt's father gave him the job of guiding drunks, which he regards as a "mission").

> It's a world of hurt—that's the phrase we use—and things happen over here, things you just can't keep to yourself. I've seen what happens to men who try. They're consumed by what they have seen and done, **they grow obsessive, and slowly they lose sight of the job they're supposed to be doing.**

But there are other thematic passages. Here's a small one, early in the story, Kurt as narrator stepping back for a moment from guiding Mrs. Gurney to explain something about the drinking and the parties.

> And I'd noticed how, with the summer ending and Labor Day approaching, all the adults would acquire a sort of desperate, clinging manner, as if this were all going to end forever, and the good times would never be seen again. Of course I now realize that the end was just an excuse to party like maniacs. The softball tournament, the salmon

derby, the cocktails, the clambakes, the barbecues, would all happen again. They always had and they always would.

And here is a more significant passage that takes place (as is typical of the device) in a rhythmic pause after the first major plot step.

> One tip about these drunks: My opinion is that **it pays in the long run to stick as close as possible to the task at hand. We're just going home, you assure them, and tomorrow it will all be different. I've found if you stray too far from the simple goal of getting home and going to sleep, you let yourself in for a lot of unnecessary hell.** You start hearing about their whole miserable existence, and suddenly it's the most important thing in the world to fix it all up, right then. **Certain things in life can't be repaired, as in Father's situation, and that's always sad, but I believe there's nothing in life that can be remedied under the influence of half a dozen planter's punches.**

Note how the now familiar meme—sticking to the simple goal—coupled with the universal statement about life at the bottom of the passage morphs into a classic aphorism, "There's nothing in life…"

And here is yet another black hole thematic passage that comes at the end of the third section of the story, in the buildup to the seduction climax. It begins with a rhetorical question.

> "Kurt," Mrs. Gurney said, looking up at me, "do you think I'm beautiful?"
>
> I switched the sandals I was holding to the other hand. First I'll tell you what I said, and then I'll tell you what I was thinking. I said yes, and I said it immediately.

And why? Because I sensed that questions that didn't receive an immediate response fell away into silence and were never answered. They got sucked into the black hole. I'd observed this, and I knew the trick was to close the gap in Mrs. Gurney's mind, to bridge the spooky silence between the question and the answer.

Finally, there is a magnificent thematic passage during the seduction scene amid the breaking waves, again couched in character thought, with a rhetorical question, and the key touchback to the image pattern, the black lines flowing from Mrs. Gurney's eyes, and the "poised" meme, including also a reference to the running Crutchfield backfill sequence (homology). In other words, the passage is a gathering device, a tie-in line, that pulls together several recurring images and memes and sets the stage for a decisive turn.

It was then, I was sure, that her hand brushed the front of my trunks. I don't remember too much of what I was thinking, if I was, and this, this not thinking too clearly, might have been my downfall. **What is out there that indicates the right way? I might have gone down all the way. I might have sunk right there. I knew all the words for it, and they were all short and brutal. Fuck, poke, screw. A voice told me I could get away with it. Who will know the difference, the voice asked. It said, Go for it. And I knew the voice, knew it was the same voice that told Mr. Crutchfield to go ahead, fuck around. We were alone—nothing out there but the moon and the sea. I looked at Mrs. Gurney, looked into her eyes, and saw two black lines pouring out of them and running in crazy patterns down her cheeks.**
      I felt I should be gallant, or tender, and kiss Mrs. Gurney. I felt I should say something, then I felt I should be quiet. It seemed as if the moment were

poised, as if everything were fragile, and held together with silence.

Thematic Passages in "Shiloh"

In "Shiloh," an idle, perennially stoned long haul truck driver decides to repair his threadbare marriage by building his wife a log cabin, which she doesn't want (she wants neither the log cabin nor the marriage); via a thematic passage, this becomes a meditation on the mystery of marriage, the loss of a child, and the damage done when neither are attended to. Some critics used to call Bobbie Ann Mason's style "K-Mart realism," or else she was thought of as a typical American minimalist of her generation, both sensationally short-sighted claims. Mason is a very complex and knowing writer, fully in command of a number of devices of structure and elaboration, despite the fact that she sets her stories in the American lower midwest amongst characters that a certain class of reader might assume to be inarticulate.

The thematic passages are surprisingly eloquent and revealing. The longest occurs right at the end of the story, after Norma Jean has told Leroy she's leaving him. This is in character thought, Leroy's mind.

> Leroy takes a lungful of smoke and closes his eyes as Norma Jean's words sink in. He tries to focus on the fact that thirty-five hundred soldiers died on the grounds around him. He can only think of that war as a board game with plastic soldiers. Leroy almost smiles, as he compares the Confederates' daring attack on the Union camps and Virgil Mathis's raid on the bowling alley. General Grant, drunk and furious, shoved the Southerners back to Corinth, where Mabel and Jet Beasley were married years later, when Mabel was still thin and good-looking. The next day, Mabel and Jet visited the battleground, and

then Norma Jean was born, and then she married Leroy and they had a baby, which they lost, and now Leroy and Norma Jean are here at the same battleground. Leroy knows he is leaving out a lot. **He is leaving out the insides of history. History was always just names and dates to him. It occurs to him that building a house out of logs is similarly empty—too simple. And the real inner workings of a marriage, like most of history, have escaped him. Now he sees that building a log house is the dumbest idea he could have had.** It was clumsy of him to think Norma Jean would want a log house. It was a crazy idea. He'll have to think of something else, quickly. He will wad the blueprints into tight balls and fling them into the lake. Then he'll get moving again.

It's typical of Leroy to think of large issues in terms of toys, models, and kits. So the analogy of war to a board game isn't surprising and yet reminds the reader of Leroy's limitations. Then he launches into a rehearsal of the story so far—Mabel's marriage and honeymoon, Norma Jean's birth, their own marriage, Randy's birth and death, but much is left out. This leads him to a complex analogy between history and marriage and his own behaviour toward Norma Jean, his ignorance of the "insides" of things, the emptiness of his notions, and the vanity of his log cabin idea. In this moment, the inarticulate Leroy has reached a fine pitch of articulation, just before he lapses back into denial and fecklessness, before the dust ruffle draws a veil.

The pattern for this is actually set earlier in the story, a moment of profundity ending with a return to vacuousness.

Leroy used to tell hitchhikers his whole life story—about his travels, his hometown, the baby. He would end with a question:"Well, what do you think?" It was just a rhetorical question. In time, he had the feeling that he'd been telling the same story over and over to the same hitchhikers. He quit talking to hitchhikers when he realized how his voice sounded—whining and self-pitying, like some teenage-tragedy song. Now Leroy has the sudden impulse to tell Norma Jean about himself, as if he had just met her. They have known each other so long they have forgotten a lot about each other. They could become reacquainted. But when the oven timer goes off and she runs to the kitchen, he forgets why he wants to do this.

And here is the thematic passage near the beginning of the story just after the initial backfill announcement of the loss of the couple's baby. Same pattern: profundity ending in vacuity and irony.

They never speak about their memories of Randy, which have almost faded, but now that Leroy is home all the time, they sometimes feel awkward around each other, and Leroy wonders if one of them should mention the child. He has the feeling that they are waking up out of a dream together—that they must create a new marriage, start afresh. They are lucky they are still married. Leroy has read that for most people losing a child destroys the marriage—or else he heard this on *Donahue*. He can't always remember where he learns things anymore.

The reader might and should be surprised to note that Leroy is neither stupid nor inarticulate in his thoughts. He is quite able to sum up the problem in their marriage, the long silence between them after the death of the child, and the necessity of a fresh start, a renewal. He even knows Norma Jean doesn't want him to build her a log cabin. But he persists in a state of hopeful denial and feckless inaction while Norma Jean is already in motion and on her way to somewhere else in life.

There is one other notable, quick thematic passage at the end of the second backfill section dealing with the baby's death.

It opens with another rhetorical question. Indeed, this is one of those thematic passages that go no farther than opening up the question. And again, note that in every one of Leroy's thematic passages we find the same rhetorical cycle: a moment of realization, an intimation of the truth, ending with a return to easy thinking and denial. I would add that this is standard operating procedure for presenting a character of two minds, someone torn between two ideas. In this case, Leroy is torn between his own ability to articulate the truth and his impulse to denial, to let the time pass, and he performs this inner conflict every time he thinks deeply about what is happening to him.

> Leroy remembers Norma Jean standing catatonically beside him in the hospital and himself thinking: Who is this strange girl? He had forgotten who she was. Now scientists are saying that crib death is caused by a virus. Nobody knows anything, Leroy thinks. The answers are always changing.

Thematic Passages in "Brokeback Mountain"

In "Brokeback Mountain," authorial parsimony and a pair of cowboys mute in the face of their shared cultural homophobia mean that the thematic passages are neither as long nor as eloquent as those in "The Point" and "Shiloh." They are terse (thematic telegrams) or delivered partly in dialogue, yet they manage to achieve a surprising universality in terms of suffering and stoic acceptance. At the end of the summer on the mountain, a storm scatters their sheep, which blend with other flocks nearby, creating an occasion for a thematic parallel.

> Even when the numbers were right Ennis knew the sheep were mixed. **In a disquieting way everything seemed mixed.**

To which situation Ennis is generally reticent in his suffering except at the very end of the story when Proulx gives us his stoicism glossed by the narrator:

> There was some open space between what he knew and what he tried to believe, **but nothing could be done about it, and if you can't fix it you've got to stand it.**

This echoes an earlier snippet of dialogue (meme), something Ennis says to Jack during their climactic dialogue scene by the Hail Strew River.

> "I goddamn hate it that you're goin a drive away in the mornin and I'm goin back to work. But **if you can't fix it you got a stand it,**" he said. "Shit. I been lookin a people on the street. This happen to other people? What the hell do they do?"

Ennis's laconic stoicism and the impossibility of achieving his hopes, the space between his love for Jack and his terror of tire irons, is the moral of the story. But that gap, the actual shape of their problem, is a process of constant triangulation without a specific answer. Twice they have a dialogue about whether they are gay or not, both times coming up in the negative. First, that summer on the mountain pastures:

> . . . but saying not a goddamn word except once Ennis said, **"I'm not a queer," and Jack jumped in with "Me neither. A one-shot thing."**

Later, during the middle act, sitting in their motel room, they talk it over again, but this time the conversation is extended to the question of whether they think of sleeping with other men (later, in the last act, this becomes a life and death question because of Jack's questionable trips to Mexico). I quote the extended passage here because of the way the text yokes the Brokeback Mountain image pattern with the question of what they are and the question of what they should do about this unsayable problem. It is in the nature of thematic passages not necessarily to answer questions but to probe them or answer them provisionally.

> Ennis pulled Jack's hand to his mouth, took a hit from the cigarette, exhaled. "Sure as hell seem in one piece to me. You know **I was sittin up there all that time tryin to figure out if I was—? I know I ain't. I mean here we both got wives and kids, right? I like doin it with women, yeah, but Jesus H., ain't nothin like this.** I never had no thoughts a doin it with another guy except I sure wrang it out a hunderd times thinkin about you. You do it with other guys, Jack?"
>
> "Shit no," said Jack, who had been riding more than bulls, not rolling his own. "You know that. **Old Brokeback got us good and it sure ain't over. We got a work out what the fuck we're goin a do now.**"

I quote both these passages—and others like them—not to be repetitious but to show that authors actually repeat significant texts—memes—and bits of structure (homologous actions) and image tags or memes for emphasis, to be clear, to guide the reader, to remind the reader that this is what the story is about. Stories insist on their meaning by creating a shimmering structure of repetitive material.

Here is a piece of thematic text, part-dialogue and part-narrative.

> [Jack] "**But fuck-all has worked the way I wanted. Nothin ever came to my hand the right way.**" Without getting up he threw deadwood on the fire, **the sparks flying up with their truths and lies**, a few hot points of fire

landing on their hands and faces, not for the first time, and they rolled down into the dirt. **One thing never changed: the brilliant charge of their infrequent couplings was darkened by the sense of time flying, never enough time, never enough.**

"Nothin ever came to hand in the right way" echoes Ennis's uneasy feeling back on the mountain when a hailstorm drives neighbouring flocks together.

Even when the numbers were right Ennis knew the sheep were mixed. **In a disquieting way everything seemed mixed.**

But the most beautiful thematic text occurs in that retrospective look in Jack's point of view after the two part company for the last time. I included this text in the image pattern loading section, but it's a thematic passage as well and bears repeating here.

What Jack remembered and craved in a way he could neither help nor understand was the time that distant summer on Brokeback when Ennis had come up behind him and pulled him close, the silent embrace satisfying some shared and sexless hunger. . . Later, the dozy embrace solidified in his memory as **the single moment of artless, charmed happiness in their separate and difficult lives.**

Which echoes on a larger scale the brief, significant slip of commentary when Jack's postcard comes to Ennis after a four-year lapse: ". . . the first **sign of life** in all that time." The point being that willy-nilly the thematic passages in a text will signal the larger meaning of life and define the reader's perspective on the action as a symbolic construct. Whatever their fears and sufferings, the cowboys' love is judged on the side of life.

Backfill, Shaping the Past

Backfill ought to be simple (just what happened before the story action) but turns out to be a highly constructed, recursive element of form. First of all, it's very focused. In "The Point," the backfill focuses on Kurt's father's suicide, plus, in a different key, Crutchfield's suicide (homology). In "Shiloh," it's the death of the baby. In "Brokeback Mountain," it's primarily the story of Ennis's cruel, homophobic father, the tire iron, and the corpse of the beaten rancher. The way the backfill is integrated into the time flow of the narrative is also important, as is the orchestration of repeated references to the background story. Simplified, the pattern generally involves one large section of backfill text and then repeated references to the backfill spread throughout the story. In other words, the backfill is less a mass of background material than it is another pattern in the story network.

Backfill in "The Point"

As I have already said, the backfill insertion in "The Point" is unusual. It comes at the end of the story, after the actual plot has technically reached closure. Kurt gets Mrs. Gurney home and tucked in, then he returns to his own house, can't sleep, retrieves a letter his father wrote from Vietnam, goes out to a swing set on the beach and reads the letter, then recalls how he discovered his father's body.

The letter is significant because it gives evidence of an early-stage dysfunctional marriage between Kurt's parents, but most of it relates the story of the father's failure to save a terribly wounded comrade. Near the end of the letter there are lines (a meme) that link directly to the theme of the story, the theory of the black hole and Kurt's method of handling Mrs. Gurney.

> They're consumed by what they have seen and done, **they grow obsessive, and slowly they lose sight of the job they're supposed to be doing.**

The description of the father's corpse and Kurt's reaction isn't a surprise for the reader. We already know that the father shot himself. The lengthier treatment adds brutal detail and one salient fact, that it was Kurt who discovered the body. But the basic news is announced in the first paragraph of the story.

> When Father was alive, she [Kurt's mother] rarely drank, but after **he shot himself** you could say she really let herself go.

A few pages later, we find a paragraph-long expansion. Mrs. Gurney sings a couple of lines of a song, which triggers Kurt's memories.

> I vaguely recalled that as a song from my parents' generation. It reminded me of **my father who shot himself in the head one morning—did I already say this? He was sitting in the grass parking lot above the Point.** Officially, his death was ruled an accident, a "death by misadventure," and everyone believed that he had in fact been cleaning his gun, but Mother told me otherwise one night...

(Note the echo, parallel, homology, with Crutchfield's suicide story, claimed to be an accidental drowning.)

There are other references to Kurt's father's suicide including one tacit, and very sad, reference after Mrs. Gurney threatens to kill herself.

[Kurt] "That won't get you anywhere."

"It'll show them."

"You'd just be dead, Mrs. Gurney. Then you'd be forgotten."

"Crutchfield isn't forgotten. Poor Crutchfield. The flag's at half-mast."

"This year," I said. "Next year it'll be back where it always was."

"My boys wouldn't forget."

That was certainly true, I thought, but I didn't want to get into it.

And another occurs in the thematic passage on "the task in hand" quoted above. "Certain things in life can't be repaired, as in my father's situation, and that's always sad." There are actually three suicides (homologous actions) in the story, Kurt's father, Crutchfield, and, potentially, Mrs. Gurney who twice threatens to kill herself. Suicide is itself a pattern that evolves out of the father backfill and forces the father's suicide into the Crutchfield story and the Mrs. Gurney plot.

Kurt's father is further linked to the plot structure and theme by the fact that it was the father who first assigned him the job of guiding the drunks home. This is mentioned in another paragraph-long backfill segment on the second page of the story. Here are the closing sentences.

> Father, who'd been a medic in Vietnam, made it my job when I was ten, and at thirteen I considered myself a hard-core veteran, treating every trip like a mission.

The Crutchfield material is backfill, also, as I say, about a suicide, and another story of Kurt leading a drunk home after a party (homology, rhyming action—the reader should be getting the heady feeling that there are dazzling and dizzying amounts of repetition going on in a good short story).

Earlier that summer, Mr. Crutchfield, the insurance lawyer, had fallen overboard and drowned while hauling in
his crab trap.

In one of her moments of resistance, Mrs. Gurney ends up
on the boardwalk in front of the Crutchfields' house. "Poor
Crutchfield," moans Mrs. Gurney. This prompts Kurt to recall
for the reader how bad the Crutchfield marriage was and
that he had once told Crutchfield it was okay to fuck around
(like suicide, bad marriages replicate and dominate the adult
relationships in the story). This passage ends with the usual
repetition of the task in hand meme, linking the Crutchfield
backfill to the Mrs. Gurney plot and to Kurt's father's letter
from Vietnam.

> He was drunk, he was miserable, and **I had a job, and
> that job was to get him home and try to prevent him
> from dwelling too much on himself.**

Even more to the point, the text, as it continues, ties Crutchfield to the theory of the black hole.

> It was that night, the night I took Mr. Crutchfield home,
> as I walked back to our house, that I developed the theory
> of the black hole…

Then there is the bit of text quoted above, after Mrs. Gurney's
suicide threat—her remark about Crutchfield not being forgotten. And, finally, in the climactic seduction scene, Crutchfield returns one more time.

> Fuck, poke, screw. A voice told me I could get away with it.
> Who would know the difference, the voice asked. It said,
> Go for it. And I knew the voice, knew it was **the same voice
> that told Mr. Crutchfield to go ahead, fuck around.**

I quote you all these textual moments because it's important to see the frequency and precision involved in running successful backfill patterns. It is equally important to see how explicitly they are inked, linked, pinned, welded into other patterns within the text by virtue of repeated memes, tags and parallel gestures. This is the net of internal reference the density of which creates the power and focus of a literary text.

Backfill in "Shiloh"

The backfill in "Shiloh" focuses on the death of the baby, Randy, some years before the present plot of the story. The baby's death is the reason Leroy's house is not a home, the reason he and Norma Jean have been running on parallel tracks for years while he drove his rig. The fact that he now stays home only throws into relief the routinized emptiness of their relationship.

In "Shiloh," as I said earlier, the backfill is displayed somewhat more conventionally than in "The Point," distributed in two segments in the first third of the story. The first passage occurs just after the opening plot conflict text and the "rustic Nativity scene" phrase. It's just a line embedded in a bit of memory and thematic material (compare with the terse announcement of Kurt's father's suicide in the first paragraph of "The Point").

> Perhaps he reminds her too much of the early days of their marriage, before he went on the road. **They had a child who died as an infant, years ago**. They never speak about their memories of Randy, which have almost faded, but now that Leroy is home all the time, they sometimes feel awkward around each other, and Leroy wonders if one of them should mention the child... They are lucky they are still married. Leroy has read that for most people

losing a child destroys the marriage—or else he heard this on *Donahue.*

A little later, in the drug dealing scene with Stevie Hamilton, we find a more detailed description of the baby's death. Note how the passage moves from Stevie's age, which links him with Randy, to the death scene (and, again, compare this scene with the scene of Kurt's father's death; both are what you might call necessary scenes).

Stevie's father was two years ahead of Leroy in high school. Leroy is thirty-four. He married Norma Jean when they were both eighteen, and their child Randy was born a few months later, but he died at the age of four months and three days. **He would be about Stevie's age now. Norma Jean and Leroy were at the drive-in, watching a double feature *(Dr. Strangelove* and *Lover Come Back)*, and the baby was sleeping in the back seat. When the first movie ended, the baby was dead. It was the sudden infant death syndrome. Leroy remembers handing Randy to a nurse at the emergency room, as though he were offering her a large doll as a present. A dead baby feels like a sack of flour. "It just happens sometimes," said the doctor, in what Leroy always recalls as a nonchalant tone.** Leroy can hardly remember the child anymore, but **he still sees vividly a scene from *Dr. Strangelove* in which the President of the United States was talking in a folksy voice on the hot line to the Soviet premier about the bomber accidentally headed toward Russia. He was in the War Room, and the world map was lit up. Leroy remembers Norma Jean standing catatonically beside him in the hospital and himself thinking: Who is this strange girl? He had forgotten who she was.** Now scientists are saying that crib death is caused by a virus. Nobody knows anything, Leroy thinks. The answers are always changing.

That's the most substantial piece of information about Randy, but as with Kurt's father and the suicide meme, the baby keeps showing up as the story develops. In his *Star Wars* needlepoint scene, Leroy recalls that, "When the baby died, she [Mabel] said that fate was mocking her." Later he recalls his truck-driving days and how he used to tell random hitchhikers his life story.

> Leroy used to tell hitchhikers his whole life story—about his travels, his hometown, **the baby.** He would end with a question: "Well, what do you think?" It was just a rhetorical question. In time, he had the feeling that he'd been telling the same story over and over to the same hitchhikers.

And a day later, Mabel turns up in her role as plot nudge and hilariously tells the story of the "datsun dog" that killed a baby.

> As soon as Norma Jean switches off the vacuum, Mabel says in a loud voice, "Did you hear about the datsun dog that killed the baby?"
>
> Norma Jean says, "The word is 'dachshund.'"
>
> "They put the dog on trial. It chewed the baby's legs off. The mother was in the next room all the time." She raises her voice. "They thought it was neglect."
>
> Norma Jean is holding her ears.

The word "neglect" particularly hurts Norma Jean. "The very idea, her bringing up the subject like that! Saying it was neglect." But the upshot is to push Norma Jean deeper into her self-improvement program; she starts night school and begins writing courses.

The last baby reference occurs in the long thematic passage at the story's close, in the potted story summary Leroy rehearses in his mind before declaring that he is leaving out a lot, leaving out "the insides of history."

Backfill in "Brokeback Mountain"

There is a bit of general background relating the hard-scrabble upbringing of the two cowboys in the setup paragraphs leading to their employment as sheepherders, but the significant backfill is actually delivered by Ennis in dialogue and this occurs in that motel room in 1967 when Ennis and Jack get together for the second time. Jack expresses his desire for the two of them to buy a ranch. Ennis responds:

> "Whoa, whoa, whoa. It ain't goin to be that way. We can't. I'm stuck with what I got, caught in my own loop. Can't get out of it. Jack, I don't want to be like them guys you see around sometimes. And I don't want to be dead. **There was these two old guys ranched together down home, Earl and Rich—Dad would pass a remark when he seen them. They was a joke even if they was pretty tough old birds. I was what, nine years old and they found Earl dead in an irrigation ditch. They'd took a tire iron to him, spurring him up, drug him around by his dick until it pulled off, just bloody pulp. What the tire iron done looked like pieces of burned tomato all over him, nose torn down from skiddin on gravel."**
> "You seen that?"
> **"Dad made sure I seen it. Took me to see it. Me and K. E. Dad laughed about it. Hell, for all I know he done the job.** If he was alive and was to put his head in that door right now you bet he'd get his tire iron. Two guys livin together? No. All I can see is we get together once in a while way the hell out in the back a nowhere."

This is a fascinating instance of the backfill form, delivered in dialogue in a scene on the plot line. Its significance is in its focus, the way it dramatically articulates the past event that motivates Ennis's plot resistance. There is a generalized aura of homophobia expressed in the cowboys' denial that they are gay, but this segment of backfill—the giving of the father law—nails Ennis's absolute terror of being outed. His expressed desire not to be dead is not abstract. Notice, as well, how Proulx attaches an image—tire iron—to the idea of homophobic rage and murder. The image, mentioned twice, becomes a pattern that achieves a kind of evil radiance when Ennis meets Jack's father and subsequently dreams that Dali-esque spoon/tire iron at the very end of the story. It's important to see how, in a short story, text is rarely univocal but hooks into the story network in multiple ways; in this case, backfill hooks into plot and image pattern and connects to other texts later in the story by parallelism (two homophobic murders, example of homology) and simple repetition of the image (forcing).

Proulx works hard to present the cowboys as a balanced pair. So she writes in a symmetrical bit of backfill for Jack involving a horrendous (and homoerotic) punishment for bedwetting (the father beats his son and then pees on him). This comes near the end of the story, when Ennis finally meets Jack's father. It's inserted as a memory Ennis has of a story Jack once told him. And it's hard-linked to the backfill about old Earl's murder by the tire iron image.

> So now he knew it had been the **tire iron**. He stood up, said you bet he'd like to see Jack's room, recalled one of Jack's stories about this old man...

These two passages of backfill speak to one another across the story text, both stories of insanely harsh fathers laying down the law, both homoerotic in their violence (pulling off old Earl's penis; peeing on a son). This is exactly the quality of internal cross-reference and rhyme that composes an artistic text (when analyzed carefully, a so-called realistic story becomes less and less realistic and more an arrangement of devices and patterns).

Envoi, on the Economy of Recirculation

The three stories I've been discussing have core similarities, which, I submit, are the core structures of narrative form. There are certainly other types of stories, for example, microstories that like aphorisms distil form and inflect it with irony and implication or experimental stories that invert or subvert conventional form (though they are always in conversation with it). And there are also myriad more or less conventional structures I have not talked about that will alter the presentation of form; for example, frame stories and observer narrators, the false document device, the pre-story, and, especially in longer works such as novels, the subplot. There are also ingenious ways of varying the core form. For example, James Joyce in "The Dead" shows Gabriel, his protagonist, in conflict with three different women in sequence. But he realized that plot only requires that the conflict stay the same (homology), while the antagonist can change. (Alice Munro, following Joyce, does the same thing in her story "Baptizing.") These devices and variants alter and complicate the presentation, but they do not depart essentially from the strictures of form.

Even so-called conventionally realistic short stories exhibit an uncommon degree of aesthetic patterning based on an economy of recirculation. The conflict formula (desire and resistance) repeats (the same action—homology; often the same text—meme) along the plot line. Images repeat, accumulate meaning, and ramify, and the branch images repeat and reconnect. Thematic passages repeat memes, reflect one another. Actions repeat other actions. The effect is not an endlessly new creation, five thousand or so different words in a row, but a story matrix, a network structure of repetitions, correlations, parallels, homologies, links, and echoes carefully focused on a limited set of story inventions that circulate. The effect is to create a symbolic action, a plot, that often seems ridiculously finite and limited—take Mrs. Gurney home, build Norma Jean a log cabin, live with the man you love—but accumulates moral significance and a stern universality with the churning reflective material.

All of which begs a question: Where does form come from? Mysterious, perhaps unanswerable. Not many people, even writers, can describe form, but they can sense what "works." Even more astonishing, readers, the countless story consumers, know form without consciously knowing it. This is a good story, that's not a good story: they can decide without any but the vaguest of ideas where their criteria derive from.

It has always struck me, though, that the basis of form is recursion, which has its roots in rhythm, eros, and memory (memorization), and that the basics of form extend back in human history, long, long before the invention of writing and our current state of historical understanding. We've been writing down stories since the Sumerians. Prior to that, for tens of thousands of years, we told them over hearth fires, accompanied perhaps by drums, flute, and lyre, dance or call-and-response chants (you can imagine all the possibilities because many cultures still deploy such rhythmic performances today). That's a hundred thousand years or more of storytellers and audience practicing together, hammering out form and response in an endless feedback loop, which, one speculates, has hard-wired the brain. The reader knows without knowing.

The other thing to notice about all three stories I've been discussing is their capacity to use form, not to moralize (although there are moral components) but to open themselves to mystery. All three stories reach a plot climax and an end—Mrs. Gurney is home and Kurt's father is dead, Norma Jean is leaving Leroy, as everyone, including Leroy, always knew she would, Jack is dead and nothing remains to Ennis except his hot memories of Brokeback Mountain. Yet the end in all three stories is a character, alone, looking (bleakly) into an infinite enigma. The story is over, the events, the agon of plot, have brought him to the edge of despair, the limit of what he can endure, and yet he is still standing, casting an eye over the ruins and wondering.

The reader possesses all the pertinent facts and reasons, but the general, essentially human, Job-like questions remain: How the Hell did I get here and why have all these things happened to me? This is what form does. It offers complexity over reduction. It opens vistas and poses larger questions than are strictly presented in the text. The entire structure of a story is rendered symbolic far beyond the finite surface plot and the insistence of theme. The complex resonating structure of form achieves spiritual lift-off. It re-situates both reader and character onto the plane of epic grandeur, under the sign of Death, and gives meaning to suffering while simultaneously annihilating meaning.

THE ART
OF NECESSITY
TIME CONTROL IN
NARRATIVE PROSE

1. Overture: On the Pervasiveness of Time Control

ONE OF THE KEYS to the density of textual effect and reverberation necessary to the creation of artistic prose is the strict use of time control. Time control is not one of the sexy topics of literary craft, things like symbols, plot, or characterization; as technique, time control is often disregarded as being unartful and mechanical, necessary, perhaps, but inelegant. For most readers, time control devices fade into the background of the wall of text, about as exciting as articles and prepositions. Words like "when," "after," "before," and "now" are prosy little road signs that subtly modify the surrounding text but are not the text itself, sharing neither the clashing drama of an active verb nor the visionary substance of a concrete noun. But to read so ingenuously is to miss the point; narrative is a temporal art (an oft-repeated though mostly unexamined truism); time control is its essence, and good authors spend a surprising portion of their texts watching the clock.

You'll discover that this chronology will have little to do with the sequence in which the events are mentioned on the page. No novel, story, or essay is written in strict chronological order. The beauty of narrative prose that uses effective time control is that you can rhumba back and forth in time, you can fracture time, you can compress time, you can skip the tedious and inconsequential times, and you can make a single imagined scene stand for a series. The key is that the time control must be clear, precise, and pervasive. Every bit of text has to carry a time signature, and when this is written properly, the reader speeds through the sentences without noticing the art.

With any new text I follow a reading practice that includes two questions about time control that help me situate myself in the textu(r)al matrix (as I think of it). What is the base tense? By base tense, I mean the primary narrative tense to which all other verb tenses in the text must relate in a clear, logical way. And what is the time flow structure? By time flow structure, I mean an analysis of the global orchestration or reshaping of the chronology, that is, the base chronology plus the artistic distribution of events in the text. How is the base chronology rearranged—scrambled, foregrounded, elided, summarized, backgrounded—in the actual text?

In a short story, for example, you generally find a forward-moving plotline combined with reference to earlier events, backfill. Conventionally, a chunk of backfill comes after a bit of introductory text or scene. In an essay or memoir, the time structure is often dual, a narrator looking back from the time-of-the-writing at an earlier episode. Individual authors vary these conventional structures in particular ways, and within the larger structures, sentence by sentence, phrase by phrase, the authors are dancing with time.

Now look at the opening of Ted Kooser's essay "Small Rooms in Time."

Several years ago, a fifteen-year-old boy answered the side door of a house where I once lived, and was murdered, shot twice by one of five people—two women and three men—who had gone there to steal a pound of cocaine. The boy died just inside the door, at the top of the staircase that led to the cellar where I had once set up my easel and painted. The robbers—all but one still in their teens—stepped over the body, rushed down the steps, and shot three people there, a woman and two men.

Somebody called the police, perhaps the people who rented the apartment on the second floor. The next day's front-page story reported that the three in the basement were expected to survive. The boy's father, who was somewhere on the first floor and out of the line of fire, had not been injured.

It's taken me a long time to try to set down my feelings about this incident. At the time, it felt as if somebody had punched me in the stomach, and in ways it has taken me until now to get my breath back. I am ashamed to say that it wasn't the boy's death that so disturbed me, but the fact that it happened in a place where my family and I had once been safe.

I recently spent most of a month building a Christmas surprise for my wife, a one-inch to one-foot scale replica of her ancestral home in the Nebraska sandhills. The original, no longer owned by her family, was a sprawling fourteen-room, two-story house built in 1884. Her grandparents and great-grandparents lived there. Her great aunt, still living and 108 years old at the time I am writing this, was born there. Her father and his brothers and sisters chased through those rooms as small children, and as a girl my wife and her young sister spent summers there, taking care of their invalid grandmother.

Four short paragraphs dense with time shifts and incident, a bravura performance. Note that the base chronology
stretches from 1884 to the present (or at least the present
as of the time-of-the-writing). The base tense is the present
tense, the present of the time-of-the-writing, from which
Kooser observes and orchestrates the past. There are five time
sequences in play: 1) The murder of the fifteen-year-old boy
(past tense); 2) An earlier period when Kooser and his family
lived in the house where the boy was later killed (pluperfect);
3) A long stretch of time focused on Kooser's wife's family and
their ancestral home (past tense); 4) Kooser "recently" building a replica of that ancestral home (past tense); 5) The stretch
of very recent time that Kooser spent coming to terms with
the news of the boy's murder leading up to the time-of-the-
writing (present tense). Time structure: [1884 to the present
(the time Kooser lived in the murder house) (the murder)
{coming to terms (building the replica) (writing the essay)}].

Within these large scale time frames there are yet smaller
step-backs. For example, the pluperfect subordinate clause
"who had gone there to steal" in the murder sequence. Note
also the use of character ages as sequence and duration indicators. A good deal of the dramatic effect of the text has to do
with Kooser's deft time control and his ability to collapse and
juxtapose the different time frames. Yet nothing in the text
goes beyond my list of homely time switch devices, adverbs,
adverbial fragments, and conjunctions.

Note how the chronological order of events (base chronology) does not reflect the order in which they appear in the
essay. This is what narratologists call anachrony. The chronological order of events mentioned in the essay is as follows:

1) 1884 building of the ancestral home
2) The generations of family occupancy
3) The great-aunt's 108 years, still going on
4) Wife's childhood summers at the ancestral home

5) Period Kooser's family spent in the murder house
6) The murder
7) Building the replica of the ancestral home
8) The time-of-the-writing

But the order in the text is different:

1) The murder (6)
2) Period Kooser's family spent in the murder house (5)
3) Time-of-the-writing (8)
4) Building the replica (7)
5) 1884, building the ancestral home (1)
6) Generations of occupancy (2)
7) Great-aunt's 108 years (3)
8) Wife's childhood summers at the ancestral home (4)

Farther down in the essay, the reader will find an example of the meta-text technique. Kooser writes:

> I could build a miniature of that house, using the approximate measurements of memory, and as I worked with plywood and paper and glue I would be able to gradually remember almost everything about it. But I won't need to do that; since the murder I often peered into those little rooms where things went good for us at times and bad at times. I have looked into the miniature house and seen us there as a young couple, coming and going.

In this passage, the word patterns of the replica house, memory, and time converge. Time experienced subjectively as memory is identified with the metaphorical small rooms of the unbuilt replica of the murder house, and Kooser equates the temporal orchestration of his essay (its anachrony) with the imaginary replica (replica of memory) of the rooms into which he peers, now this one, now that. Such reflexive self-commentary is more common than the common reader expects and notices. Writers, contrary to conventional wisdom, do like to explain what they are doing.

4. The Theory of Globs

When I was young and trying to teach myself to write (a long and unfinished process), I used to gorge on craft books. One of the certainties I imbibed was that narrative prose divides into scene and summary. Scene is present, happening action often with dialogue, very cinematic. Summary fills in the past or compresses stretches of time. Time moves slowly in the scene but quickly in summary. *Techniques of Fiction Writing: Measure and Madness* by Leon Surmelian was one of the craft books that particularly struck me. And it's not bad as these books go; Surmelian was an honest seeker. But he just slaughtered me as a beginning writer with advice like this:

> One of the first things a writer must do in organizing his material is to place his scenes and summaries. He has to decide in advance what goes into scene and what goes into summary and work out his scene line and summary line.

After reading that, I would dutifully block out my scenes, then insert a chunk of summary, then a scene and more summary and so on. The result was moribund, ponderous, monotonous, and mechanical. I felt like I was juggling elephants.

So I went to the library, rifled the fiction shelves, tried first to find the scenes and summary, then realized that the concepts scene and summary don't actually work as monolithic compositional devices. How, for example, can you make a useful distinction between scene and summary in any of the examples I've already discussed? They are a mishmash of scene, suggested scene, scene snippets, description, actions, memory, and commentary. Mishmash isn't quite the right word. If you look at, say, the last paragraph of the Ted Kooser example above, you might want to call it summary, but that would entirely miss the writerly point, that it's a pyrotechnic spiral time nebula. It starts with a recent month (just prior to the time-of-the-writing), swirls back to 1884, compasses a century of family habitation, including the 108-year-old great-aunt, then sucks right up to the present time-of-the-writing before nodding back to the childhood summers of the author's wife. In syntactic terms, the passage is a riot of activity; next to it, the word "summary" has the drab aura of a 1950s Soviet apartment block.

What I noticed was that writers tango, foxtrot, jitterbug, jive, Charleston, tap, and waltz with time, their texts shot through with diverse rhythms and chronologies, enlivened with starts and stops and intricate folds like the cerebral cortex itself. And so I needed a different way of dividing up the text. Which is when I invented the Theory of Globs (name coined in a fit of youthful exuberance, intending to satirize the portentous Greek retro-formations of narratology, a discipline I have since learned to revere). What you find is that narrative texts, fiction or nonfiction, break at the time switches. Such divisions are precise, but it takes practice to differentiate between large structural divisions and what you might call the detailing.

So with the Kooser text above, you can make a rough but useful division at the time switches beginning with "Several years ago," which introduces two paragraphs of material about the murder (with some smaller time switches in between, the detailing). Then the present tense switch "It's taken me a long time" introduces commentary about the author's reaction to the murder. And finally the last pyrotechnic paragraph starts with the switch "I recently spent," which heralds a piece of text about his wife's ancestral home and the generations of her family. I call these large segments between the major time switches globs.

Globs are chunks of information or semantic units. They can be scenic, descriptive, swirling, or panoramic or any number of other things. Operationally, globs are defined by time shifts. That is, if you read a story or a novel or a memoir, more often than not, time indicators (before, after, etc.) or tense changes signal a movement between globs (event, backfill, thematic passage, topic, summary, etc.). A scene would be a single glob, but some long scenes can break into multiple globs. For example, Elizabeth Tennant's story "No One's a Mystery" consists of one long scene that breaks into three successive globs, each movement forward having its own dramatic unity and emotional torque.

A section of backfill could be another. A subplot segment. A thematic paragraph. A segment of thought. A piece of real summary (like a time-loop). The time-shift principle needs to be applied thoughtfully, of course. Discursive writers like Sterne or Kundera will simply shift sideways and slip into a different subject matter or train of thought. Yet even in such texts the shift of subject is often signaled by a time switch indicating simultaneity, for example, "at the same time," "similarly," "also," or some syntactic parallel.

5. Globs in Practice

Learning to read for globs and time switches is a practical skill best acquired through example. Here's the opening of my short story "Fire Drill" (from *Dog Attempts to Drown Man in Saskatoon*), tabled for analysis because it dates from when I was teaching myself the rudiments of time control, consciously applying the techniques discussed in this essay. It has the virtue of being simple—I was taking baby steps—but at the same time, I was inspired with the idea that writing fiction could be a boogie instead of a plod. I have indicated the breaks with what I call globbing lines (a quick and useful way of noting how the text breaks, which you refine even further by adding up or down arrows in the margin to indicate backfill and forward-moving action):

The bentwood rocker in our living room [[**belonged** to Aunt Maggie. Jack **refinished** it, **glued** the joints solid and **had the wicker seat re-woven for our third anniversary**. But Aunt Maggie **died** of Alzheimer's Disease]] and **sitting** in her chair **always gives** me the creepy feeling **I'll turn out** the same. "You're weirder than I thought," **says Jack**, eyeing me as if my worst fears have **already been realized**.

Time neutral setup with inset time loop.

Glob line.

Also in our living room **we have** an iron wood-burning stove, of the kind Jack **sells** out of his bicycle shop **over the winter lull**, and a giant aquarium [[**which I gave him as a graduation present. The aquarium is full** of greenish water, plastic plants and coloured pebbles, but the last Black Molly **vanished six years ago when we moved to Aurora from Toronto. For a while** it **housed** a goldfish Erin **won** at the county fair,]] but no one **has seen** "Gilda" **for months. Now** Erin **perches** on the landing above the tank and throws in pennies for wishes. **We're** the only family I know with a private wishing well in the living room. **I tell Jack he's** pretty weird himself.

Time neutral setup parallel/ simultaneous to paragraph above.

On Erin's first day of kindergarten I forget what I am doing and sit in Aunt Maggie's chair by mistake. Erin **huddles** in my lap, pale as death, unwilling to cry, taut as piano wire. **I don't know** which of us **is freaked out** the most. **Erin is freaked** out because **they pulled** a surprise fire drill on her bus **on the way home** and **it terrified her**.

Forward-moving action. Plot begins.

I'm freaked out because Erin **is freaked** out. But except for landing in Aunt Maggie's rocker **I am maintaining control.**

I am waiting for Jack to get home from the shop **before I break down** completely. This is as per my instructions from our therapist

---

Backfill.

who has deduced that I am unable to cope well in crisis situations. **Now, if anything happens** to Erin, **I keep my lips zipped** up and calmly **hand her over** to her father and **leave** the room. **Later, when the cut is cleaned and bandaged, when the bruise is kissed and the tears wiped away,** she can come to me for a hug. The **therapist says** this way **I won't turn** my daughter into a basket case **before she gets to high school.**

New backfill segment. Scene.

Naturally, **I have already phoned** Jack.

"Come right home," **I say.** "I can't handle it. She won't say a word. They stopped the bus in the middle of the road and made all the kids climb out the back. She didn't know what was happening."

"She'll be okay," **says Jack.**

- -

Nested glob. Backfill set inside backfill scene.

He is altogether too cool in a crisis. [[**A year ago** I nearly **died** hemorrhaging from an ectopic pregnancy. The orderlies **were wheeling** me into the operating room, my abdomen full of blood, tubes sprouting from my arms and nose, **and someone whispers,** "Has the husband seen her? Make sure she sees her husband before she goes under." **I know** this is the end. **I know I am going to check out** on the table. **Jack bends** over me, and **I realize that we have to make the most of this last moment together. He says,** "How does it feel to have one of those things down your nose?" **I say,** "Well it's not as bad as you might think." **Those were my last words.** At least **they could have been** my last words.]] As I say, **Jack is altogether too cool**.

- -

"How do you know she'll be okay? You can't see her. Why would they scare a kid like that?"

"It's the law," **he says.** "They do it for their own protection."

"It's a dumb law."

_____

[Extra space, arrows, notes, globbing lines, emphasis and brackets added for clarity.]

The story begins with two globs, two descriptive paragraphs of story setup. The word "also" in this instance is a time switch indicating simultaneity and parallelism, and this is reflected in the structural parallelism in the syntax. Both paragraphs contain what I call time loops into the past; they both begin in the present and end in the present with a swooping movement backwards in time. "The bentwood rocker in our living room"—present tense, an ongoing present—"belonged to Aunt Maggie"—past tense, refers to a long period of time during which Aunt Maggie had the rocker—"Jack refinished it . . . for our third anniversary"—still past but a more recent past, includes "third anniversary" time stamp—"but Aunt Maggie died of Alzheimer's Disease"—back before Jack came into possession of the chair—"sitting in her chair always gives me"—present tense, ongoing present—"'You're weirder than I thought,' says Jack"—scene snippet with dialogue, present tense but still part of an ongoing present.

Insert globbing line.

As I say, it's critical to establish the base tense because good writers are always working precisely off the base tense as an anchor point. The base tense of the story is present and all the tenses shift accordingly; so simple past denotes events before the story action. But the story is obviously in the past, has already taken place, so this is one of those artificial, "literary" or notional presents.

The second paragraph begins with "also," a time switch indicating simultaneity. "Also in the living room we have a wood burning stove"—present tense, a parallel to the ongoing present of the first paragraph—"I gave him as a graduation present . . . the last Black Molly vanished six years ago. . . For a while it housed a goldfish . . . but no one has seen "Gilda" for months"—time loop into the past as far back as Jack's graduation and up to the present, a little story about the aquarium and the family parallel to the story about the rocking chair—"Now Erin perches on the landing above the tank"—adverb "now" and present tense return us to the ongoing present—"I tell Jack he's pretty weird himself"—present tense, scenic with implied dialogue and a parallel to the last sentence of the first paragraph. (The close reader will notice that for simplicity I am not pointing out every single time shift.)

Insert globbing line.

The third paragraph begins with "On Erin's first day of kindergarten," a time switch that dumps the reader into the present forward-moving action of the story. This kind of time switch is standard operating procedure in narrative, the swinging gate between the ongoing present of the setup and a particular moment when the action starts, when crisis begins to boil. What follows is a present-tense scene with Erin sitting in her mother's lap on the rocker, and everybody is freaked out. This scene extends into the next paragraph, the fourth, and ends with the words, "This is as per my instructions from our therapist." A new glob begins with the tense change "who has deduced." There follows a segment of backfill text dealing with narrator's therapy sessions, her irrational fears, and her new coping mechanisms. This glob ends with a line that segues back to the present: "The therapist says this way I won't turn my daughter into a basket case before she gets to high school." The "therapist ... therapist" structure demonstrates how efficiently globs work in conjunction with rhetorical book-ending devices like epanalepsis.

Insert globbing line.

"Naturally, I have already phoned Jack." This line serves as a time switch (adverb "already" and tense change) to a backfill scene just moments earlier. The new scene, a telephone conversation, begins, "'Come right home,' I say." It takes place in the past, just prior to the present forward-moving action of the story. But note that after the initial tense change to the past ("I have already"), the text reverts to the present tense, a standard technique for preserving immediacy and fluidity; you can do this as long as your time switches are clear and logical; the reader will follow.

"A year ago I nearly died hemorrhaging from an ectopic pregnancy" is a time switch carrying us to another segment of backfill, deeper in the past, a sad but comic, anecdote that motivates the narrator's neurotic fears and her irritation with her husband. I indicate the glob change here with a broken line and double square brackets because—wait for it—at the end of the hospital scene, the narrative segues back out to the telephone conversation between Jack and the narrator. The structure is a glob-within-a-glob, what I call a nested glob, and though the nomenclature is intentionally whimsical, the technique is really quite common, a chunk of text, a semantic unit, nested inside another semantic unit for rhetorical effect: rhythm, dramatic juxtaposition, suspension, jazz. In this case, it makes the telephone conversation scene more interesting by the violence of interruption and by inserting helpful context. Note also the accompanying epanalepsis: "He is altogether too cool in a crisis. . . As I say, Jack is altogether too cool."

Thinking in terms of globs gives you a more or less quantitative approach to controlling certain aspects of narrative flow. For example, basic rules of proportion apply: the longer the globs, the slower the narrative rhythm; the shorter the globs, the quicker the rhythm (some narratives are waltzes, some are jigs). This is a root consideration in that mysterious literary notion of pace. Usually an author indicates in the first few lines of a story or novel what the pace will be and sticks to it. A long glob in the middle of a short-globbed story is clearly a faux pas or, at best, an anomaly that may need rethinking—it might, for example, be shortened or split up (running globs). Often globs grow shorter as the narrative approaches its climax. And there is an obvious, but useful, corollary in regard to emphasis: the longer treatment (glob) always seems more important (to the reader) than the shorter. Similarly, a repeated treatment is more important than a single instance.

The concepts of globs and anachrony speak also to the infamous backfill trap into which apprentice writers are always falling; a story or a memoir begins with a spritely scene, a teaser soon followed by a descent into a swamp of backfill out of which the narrative never ascends again, or only fitfully. Backfill can and probably should be broken up and distributed rather than delivered in one lump (the effect of which is to make the narrative look like a snake that has swallowed a horse). Globs are modular. Think of the way newspaper editors once actually cut stories into segments with scissors and pasted them back together again in a new order. This can be done just as easily with fiction or memoir. Globs can be repeated. Or, once entered in the text, they may be referred to over and over, bringing the whole back into the reader's mind without necessarily going through the entire sequence of words again.

Globs may be organized in patterns of light and dark (comedy and tragedy) or in patterns of increasing poetic intensity (rising to a climax). Repetition and patterning, combined with globbing (yes, there is a verb "to glob") for pace, helps to give a piece of writing a rhythmic quality. Globs can also be varied in length so as to give an effect of syncopation. Writing becomes a dance under a strobe, quicksilver flashes of movement, like the flashes of sunlight in Annie Dillard's text, instead of that awkward shuffle of scene and summary.

6. Thought Points

Then/Now Construction: This is a lovely and common device (though little noticed as such) for juxtaposing two time periods as a syntactic unit. The juxtaposition itself dramatizes the changes that have taken place over time, tells a story, but in a very short space, eliding all the time in between. Thomas Wyatt's poem "They Flee From Me" begins with alternating then/now constructions.

> They flee from me that sometime did me seek
> With naked foot, stalking in my chamber.
> I have seen them gentle, tame, and meek,
> That now are wild and do not remember
> That sometime they put themself in danger
> To take bread at my hand; and now they range,
> Busily seeking with a continual change.

Future tense: The narrative assumption, even in the tricky case of the present tense, is that the events presented in a text have already taken place. The future is either prophecy or projection. It speaks to character motivation. What does the character want? What is his or her dream of the future? What does the character plan to do to achieve a goal? A beautiful example of using the future as motivation occurs in *Henry V* in the St. Crispin's Day speech:

> He that outlives this day, and comes safe home,
> Will stand a tip-toe when this day is nam'd,
> And rouse him at the name of Crispian.
> He that shall live this day, and see old age,
> Will yearly on the vigil feast his neighbours,
> And say "To-morrow is Saint Crispian."
> Then will he strip his sleeve and show his scars,
> And say "These wounds I had on Crispin's day."

Apocalyptic literature: The prophetic texts in the Old Testament use a cunning time control technique. The temple priests in charge of redacting older texts were able to insert accurate predictions about future events because at the time they were working, the events had already taken place. Thus Daniel is able to predict the future (to him) rise of the Medes and the Persians and their subsequent defeat by the Greeks, Alexander's death, and the coming of the Romans (all of which is history to his editors). (Daniel 7-12)

There is no rule against using this technique in fiction. In my short story "The Obituary Writer" (*A Guide to Animal Behaviour*), the present tense narration switches to future tense in the Apocalyptic mode, telling the reader what will happen to the hero.

> I will tell you now that Aiden dies. Perhaps you have already guessed it. Annie and I finally will have separated for good. I will have gone away to another city and another newspaper job. I will fly back for the funeral . . .

7. Time, Consciousness, and Verisimilitude

It's not so difficult to understand why beginning writers give short shrift to time control. We share a commonsense, unthought idea of what time is: it's like an invisible river, a flowing thing, outside us, though we're also in it in a strange way. It's like the air we breathe, yet we observe its effects—we experience boredom, things change, we get older, people die. But without thinking about it, we organize all experience in sequence, "before" always comes before "after"; if it didn't, we wouldn't have a world as we know it. If we lose the capacity to sort things in time, we descend into chaos and madness. If there is no now, no before, and no after, then where are we? Who are we?

If that's true in the real world, then it must be true in the world of literature. If the writer is not logging events in terms of time, they begin to float, they fail to cohere, to connect, they become dull and irrelevant to the reader (who is busily trying to discern sequence and duration just as he would in the real world). The text has to replicate consciousness in order to achieve verisimilitude, the quality of seeming to be real. A story can be quite unreal in other ways—as in Kafka's "The Metamorphosis" or science fiction or tales of magic or the supernatural—as long as the time control is sufficient to convince the reader that the story consciousness is observing the world of the text as the reader would.

I am always after writing students to make their texts more active, and more often than not, given that I'm a guy, they think I want a sex scene or a fistfight, which couldn't be further from the truth. What I mean is syntactic action, which could be plot or thought but generally speaking is more like that density of material and internal reference that I mentioned at the beginning of this essay and that comes from precise control of time and the balletic juxtaposition of chronologies.

In every one of the examples I've put on the table, the syntactic play of time, the way the so-called facts of the story are distributed in terms of temporal arrangement, is far more exciting than the facts alone. Proust's narrator remembers waking up early in the past. Annie Dillard's narrator is just watching fish in the sunlight. But the temporal choreography is all dash and iridescence, a flickering surface of related time frames that the reader can follow with delight, without being consciously aware of the mechanics of craft, because the author has given precise instructions in the text as to how it should be read. This is the mysterious point at which the art of necessity and the necessity of art converge.

BUILDING
SENTENCES

E NGLISH was my worst subject (next to Health) in high school, right through to my second year of university, when I stopped taking English. I'd fallen afoul of the empty rule syndrome. Don't use the pronoun "I" in an essay; don't begin sentences with "but" or "because"; write paragraphs to the topic sentence-body text-conclusion pattern (even if it bores you to death to say the same thing three times); vary sentence structure. The trouble with these rules is that no one told me why any of them would be especially useful.

"Vary sentence structure" was a rule I puzzled over for years. No one explained grammar and syntax to me well enough to make useful connections. At first I thought, well, I can write long and short sentences, something like Hemingway. Then I practiced emphatic placement of important material (at the beginning or the end of the sentence, I was told) and inversion (writing the sentence backwards—kind of fun). None of this got me anywhere because I could not join the spirit of a sentence, what emotional and factual impact I intended, with the idea of sentence structure.

I puzzled through instruction books. I discovered the wonderful distinctions between simple, compound, and complex sentences and the even more mysterious cumulative and periodic sentences. I practiced writing periodic sentences until I was blue in the face without actually being able to discover how that made them interesting for readers. They weren't very interesting to me. And my stories did not seem any better for having good topic sentence paragraphs, long and short sentences, and a scattering of lovely periodic sentences.

The rules remained irretrievably inanimate, void of life. The nexus of intention and form escaped me. Above all, the whole idea that you had to know what you were going to write before you wrote it was like a lock on my soul. It made writing drudgery.

I was writing fiction all the while and making other discoveries, for example, the fairly elementary fact that stories need drama, that they eventuate out of conflict. Not just conflicted characters, mind you. You need a character in conflict with other characters in an ongoing action. The spirit of conflict is what drives a story and illuminates character, a desire meeting a resistance. Once you have a desire (motive) and a resistance, a certain story logic follows. Spirit and form fuse. I understood this in terms of a story as a whole before I began to see that the same principle applies in sentences.

One day I happened to read an essay called "On Some Technical Elements of Style in Literature" by Robert Louis Stevenson. He was talking about sentences, but instead of repeating the platitudes, he showed how to construct sentences on the basis of conflict. Instead of just announcing a single thesis, a sentence begins by setting out two or more contrasting ideas; the sentence develops a conflict, intensifying toward a climax, a "knot" Stevenson calls it, and then, after a moment of suspension, slides easily toward a close. Suddenly, I understood both how to write those lovely lengthy compound-complex sentences and also how to write paragraphs that had nothing to do with topic sentence-body-conclusion patterns (because I could construct a paragraph the way Stevenson constructs his long sentences). Suddenly writing a sentence became an exciting prospect, a journey of discovery, a miniature story, with a conflict and a plot the outcome of which I might not know at the outset.

Simultaneously (really this all seems to have happened in a moment, a flash of personal insight), I was studying Alice Munro's short stories, trying to understand why her sentences were under contract at *The New Yorker*. What I finally noticed was Munro deploying the principle of conflict in much the same way Stevenson had, turning her clauses and sentences on the word "but" or some cognate structure (what I call a but-construction).

Here's an Alice Munro passage from "Lives of Girls and Women": "My mother had a book of operas. She would get it out and follow the story, identifying the arias, for which translations were provided. She had questions for Fern, but Fern did not know as much about opera as you would think she might; she would even get mixed up about which one it was they were listening to. But sometimes she would lean forward with her elbows on the table, not now relaxed, but alertly supported, and sing, scorning the foreign words." Four sentences, three but-constructions, and a complete inversion, at the end, of the reader's opinion of Fern.

"But" introduces the conflict, incites the plot, and opens the sentence up to a logical but unpredictable development. The "but" creates content where there was none. It creates what I call aesthetic space, into which the writer pours newly imagined, perhaps entirely surprising material. You don't have to know what you're going to write ahead of time if you understand that the sentence is an adventure not a fact, that it is less about communication than entertainment (in a deep sense), and that by creating then resolving an antithesis, the sentence invents something new, a fresh thought.

The first technique I learned and applied consciously was the list. This was in an early story "Pender's Visions" from *The Mad River and Other Stories* that begins with a line—

"Pender is a bottle, a glass, a table, a gun, a house." The line becomes a refrain through the text, only to modulate in the last section of the story into, "Pender, a bottle, a glass, a table, a gun, a house, a world."

This was, as I say, a first attempt (no apologies for being young), but you can see the rhythmic effect of a long series that becomes a structural effect by the repetition of the line throughout the text, and then becomes a thematic effect by the modulation of the series at the end. The modulation is especially significant because a series (of vaguely similar or parallel entities) creates reader expectation, and the reader always enjoys having his expectations tweaked.

Rabelais was a gargantuan list writer. In an early chapter of *Gargantua and Pantagruel,* he gives a paragraph-long list of plant matter the boy Gargantua uses to wipe his butt. "Then I wiped myself with sage, with fennel, with dill and anise, with sweet marjoram, with roses, pumpkins, with squash leaves, and cabbage, and beets, with vine leaves, and mallow, and *Verbascum thapsus* (that's mullein, and it's as red as my _____)–and mercury weed, and purslane, and nettle leaves, and larkspur and comfrey. But then I got Lombardy dysentery, which I cured by wiping myself with my codpiece."

This is complex and hilarious, hilarious because it is a long silly list that contains some very odd choices. Pumpkins? Note also that list makers pass on conventional punctuation and grammar. Instead of a series of items separated by commas right to the end, Rabelais modulates to comma-and breaks, then reverts to the earlier convention, then goes to comma-and to the close of the sentence. A lot of "ands." Rhythm is everything in a list, but you don't want the rhythm to send the reader off to sleep, so you synchopate.

Rabelais also disrupts the list with the Latin name for mullein and inserts a comical parenthetical and comments directly to the reader, creating a syntactic drama that breaks the rhythm temporarily. Then he adds a but-construction that gives the list a plot. Instead of an endless repetition of the same wiping act, the boy gets dysentery (with an ethnic slap at Lombards). Then we come back to wiping.

This is brilliant list writing because it's outrageously funny, rhythmic, and has plot. The basic principles are all there: list, rhythm, plot, and disruption (by changing up series members, by grammatical disruption, by authorial interruption, and by but-construction).

Here's another list from a somewhat later story of mine, "Heartsick," from *Dog Attempts to Drown Man in Saskatoon.* An eighty-three-year-old, love-tormented patient in an old-folks home in Austria is explaining to her psychiatrist why she is obsessed with the sixteenth-century condottiere Maleteste Baglione. "Old Maleteste (she must have said), old Bad Balls, old scamp, old scalliwag, scapegrace, turncoat, rake-hell, old *ame-de-boue*, old *passe-partout*, old rip, old fallen angel. Old white-livered poltroon. Old pessimist. Old shadow-shuffler. Old passion pit, old lust pot, old leader of men and molester of young horses. A man, in short, of incalculable zeal and confused purposes. A man, in short."

Notice again the unconventional list punctuation, the rhythmic change-ups, the comic and surprising juxtapositions, the internal rhymes, and parallel constructions. And at the end the comic list becomes a thematic list. The last four words, emphatically repeating the word "man," turn a list of comic condemnation into a generous and compassionate summation of what it means to be human.

My little list journey came full circle when I introduced Rabelais as a character in my novel *Elle*. Here is Elle reporting Rabelais' judgment on the current state of publishing (not much different from our own): "He is already tired of amateurs, retired explorers, soldiers, prelates, ambassadors, midwives, courtesans, tennis players, lovers, swordsmen, cooks, kings (not to mention the king's relatives), who all their lives read nothing but a breviary, account books, a dozen letters and an almanac or two and then sit down to write a book as if their opinions were worth more than an eel's whisker to anyone but themselves."

Obviously, you can use lists, like but-constructions, to enliven sentences and paragraphs no end (they don't all have to be comic, but it's always salutary to remember that the earliest novels, the works of Rabelais and Cervantes, were comedies). But you can also deploy a list as a larger structure, almost as substitute for plot. I recommend especially two list stories: Steven Millhauser's "The Barnum Museum" and Leonard Michaels' "In the Fifties."

Parallel construction was another one of those structures English teachers taught me in high school without also telling why it was in the least useful or beautiful. Drone, drone, eyeballs rolling back in my head; another C- on that test. Later I learned the lesson. Here is an example from Mark Anthony Jarman's great short story "Burn Man on a Texas Porch": "I'm okay, okay, will be fine except I'm hoovering all the oxygen around me, and I'm burning like a circus poster, flames taking more and more of my shape—am I moving or are they? I am hooked into fire, I am hysterical light issuing beast noises in a world of smoke."

What you have here are two sentences built on a series of parallels that invert briefly at the parenthetical em-dash and then modulate into a variant (I'm, I'm, I'm, am I, I am, I am). The simple meaning of the sentences is that the narrator is on fire. But Jarman uses parallels to throw the sentence forward in a series of waves of energy, each surge encoded with another grotesque and moving image of self-incineration. The parallels delay the end of the sentence (as the Russian Formalist Viktor Shklovsky tells us, delay is the first problem in writing a story) and create a passionately dramatic telling. Instead of mere description, the sentences become a poem.

Each new iteration of the parallel creates more of that mysterious thing I call aesthetic space, a blank spot into which the author has to imagine new and surprising words. Form never limits a writer; it creates openings for fresh invention. It also creates an opportunity for what I call narrative yoking, syntactically juxtaposing two or more ideas to create astonishing new connections or psychological parallelism.

Here is a bit from Hubert Aquin's novel *Prochain Episode*. Aquin made mad fun out of shifting from one meaning level to another with parallel constructions, shifting gears, as it were, at the commas. "I side-slip in my memory, just as I side-slipped in my Volvo in the pass through the Mosses. . ."And again from the same novel: "Laughter rose from the other table as I relaxed after my exhausting race by looking into the inert depth of the lake, by waiting to kill the time of a man whom I knew only by his ability to be someone else."

Here is a passage of multiple parallels from *The Loser*, a novel by the Austrian writer Thomas Bernhard. Using successive parallels, he links the concepts of cage, catastrophe, and perversion. "So I go from one cage to the next, Wertheimer once said, from the Kohlmarkt apartment to Traich and then back again, he said, I thought. From the catastrophic big-city cage into the catastrophic forest cage. Now I hide myself here, now there, now in the Kohlmarkt perversity, now in the country-forest perversity." And from the same novel, an example of psychological parallelism; Bernhard here contrasts Wertheimer and Glenn Gould by juxtaposing content within syntactic parallels: "Wertheimer always set about his life with false assumptions, I said to myself, unlike Glenn who always set about his existence with the right assumptions."

Finally, here is a run of parallels for dramatic and comedic effect from the beginning of my own story "Tristiana" in *Savage Love*. "He started by killing the lambs, stuffing their skins in the cracks between the sappy logs. Then he kilt the ewes, one by one, then he kilt the ram, then he kilt the ox and the riding mule which was starving also. Then he kilt his wife. And then his dog, regretting of the dog more than the rest because it was a pure Tennessee Plott Hound."

The lesson is to inject conflict, rhythm, plot, and energy into your sentences by deploying relatively simple forms: but-constructions, lists, and parallels. Never leave a lame, crude sentence snoozing on the page when there is the possibility of dramatic elaboration.

Writers create drama in sentences and paragraphs by using grammatical forms to juxtapose material with different shades of meaning. If you say, "Usually Mel's mother reminded her of a giraffe, but today she seemed more like an elephant," you force the reader to compare elephants, giraffes, and mothers and the differences between them. Power lies in the differential relation.

Here is Keats on modern love: "And what is love? It is a doll dress'd up"—a line of poetry that forces the reader to measure the distance between his idea of love and a dressed up doll. And here is an aphorism from my story "Bad News of the Heart" in *16 Categories of Desire*: "And what is love? An erotic accident prolonged to disaster."

Aphorism, epigram, and apophthegm are words that refer to roughly the same set of constructs: short, witty statements built around at least one balanced contrast. I taught myself to write them after reading Lawrence Durrell's *Alexandria Quartet*. Someone called Durrell's style lapidary; after I looked up the word, I wanted to be lapidary, too. The Greeks wrote epigrams as epitaphs, to be carved on stones over the graves of heroes, hence the term lapidary, words worth being carved in stone for the ages.

The easiest way to teach yourself how to write aphorisms is to collect an assortment from your favourite writers, group them into formal types, and map the types. "Love is an erotic accident prolonged to a disaster" is a definition type. You get a lot that begin: love is, life is, women are, the world is, and so on. "The world is but a school of inquiry." (Montaigne) "Life is always better under the influence of mild intoxicants" (from "Woman Gored by Bison Lives" in *A Guide to Animal Behavior*). Here is one I stole from a woman I dated briefly and put into a story: "Love is like the telephone—more than one can use the line" (from "Savage Love").

The predicate contrasts with the subject of the sentence, or, to be more precise, it contrasts with the common understanding of the term in the subject. Epigrams and aphorisms are always subverting the common understanding and reader expectation; their nature is to be provocative and ironic. In his *Historie of Serpents* (1608), Edward Topsall wrote: "Some learned Writers..haue compared a Scorpion to an Epigram.. because as the sting of the Scorpion lyeth in the tayle, so the force and vertue of an Epigram is in the conclusion."

A simple and fun type opens with the barefaced comparison of two or three classes: There are two kinds of _____; the one _____, and the other _____. "There are two positions available to us—either crime which renders us happy, or the noose, which prevents us from being unhappy." (de Sade) Here is one I wrote to the pattern (and sent in an email to a recalcitrant student): "There are two kinds of readers; the adventurers who glory in the breathtaking audacity and risk of a well-turned aphorism and the weenies who, lacking courage themselves, find it affront in others."

There is a type of aphorism that goes straight to the heart of the form and begins with the word difference. "The difference between pornography and literature is that in pornography everyone has orgasms all the time. There is no gap between desire and consummation. In literature there is always an element of frustration, displacement, delay and incompleteness (even if somebody does eventually manage to have an orgasm)" (from *The Enamoured Knight*).

Aphorists often write in bunches. They pick terms or term pairs and churn out variations, eventually throwing away the weaker attempts. For example, I have done a lot of form/content aphorisms. A few survived the cut. "Faith like form is content-independent." "Nostalgia is form; hope is content" (from "Dog Attempts to Drown Man in Saskatoon"). Both these aphorisms are easily imitated forms. For example, X like Y is _____. Men like cacti prefer to keep even their loved ones at a distance.

The aphorism is at once artificial and inventive. It was Nietzsche's favourite device; he called his little essays, *Versuche*, attempts, trials, stabs, but their form was epigrammatic. Theodor Adorno's *Minima Moralia* is a book of extended aphorisms in the Nietzschean mode. The French-Romanian author E. M. Cioran has published several books of aphorisms, notably *The Trouble with Being Born.* The sections of my novel *The Life Times of Captain N.* called "From Oskar's Book about Indians" are extended aphorisms based on the term pairs oral/literate and European/native.

Aphorisms are a form of thought, thought experiments. They have dash and panache. They render the author authoritative. They are the acme of the art of writing sentences. Nietzsche called them "the forms of eternity."

MAKING FRIENDS
WITH A STRANGER

ALBERT CAMUS' *L'ÉTRANGER*

WAS EIGHTEEN when I read *L'Étranger* for the first time. I read it in French in a freshman class at York University in Toronto, probably read it in English simultaneously. I think I even wrote an essay about it in French, and that essay might still exist somewhere in a box. Or possibly I dream this, trying to impress myself. I still do remember lines of poems I memorized that year: *Mignonne, allons voir si la rose / Qui ce matin avoit desclose / Sa robe de pourpre au Soleil....*

I remember the instructor, a pale, heavy-lidded young man who rarely rose from the chair behind his desk, droning on with his face in a book. He wore a shiny grey suit and a white shirt open at the neck, which I took to be Continental attire. His eyes were invariably puffy and irritated—the word *dissipated* comes to mind now. I often sat next to a girl named Karen Yolton who was also sleepy, wore black nail polish but nervously tore her cuticles, and whispered scandalous tales of her escapades in a city that was new and alien to me.

I was a little lost and amorphously rebellious and wanted desperately to be an outlaw. I got an F on my first English paper. And perhaps this bled into my reading of Camus, especially

Meursault's carefree sensuality with his lover Marie and his inarticulate defiance of conventional normative language. I remember my teenage outrage at being told to feel what I didn't feel. That was the thing you noticed in the novel as a young person—the appeal to false authority, the sense of people asking things of you that you didn't feel and you didn't feel like giving. Hell, I wanted to sleep with girls and defy authority; Meursault and I were one in my heart, aside from, you know, the small matter of shooting the Arab to death on the beach.

Somehow I always slid over the actual murder any time I summarized the novel to myself, seeing Meursault as a victim of social and linguistic tyranny not a confessed killer. Camus himself famously, and perhaps mischievously, confused his readers by saying, "In our society any man who does not weep at his mother's funeral runs the risk of being sentenced to death." This is neither an accurate description of the French criminal justice system nor the novel itself. Meursault shoots the Arab once, then pauses before pumping another four bullets into his body. Meursault's interrogation before the examining magistrate turns on this fact, for which he has no explanation. But it shreds any chance of his pleading self-defense.

I was eighteen, as I say, and enamoured with the outlaw girl I met in French class, with her ragged cuticles, cigarette rasp, and freckles, and I had no clear idea what Existentialism was except insofar as I had seen a picture of Camus, looking dour and swarthy with a cigarette in his mouth, and somehow had decided this was the very image of the Existentialist hero, a phrase I now realize is an oxymoron, and I would imagine Karen, Camus/Meursault, and myself becoming really good friends, comrades against the (adult) world.

I adopted Existentialism as an attitude rather than an idea. Though deep down I quickly divined the speciousness of its crucial ethical argument, the basic and unworkable paradox of having to create value by making decisions without recourse to values. In time, I came to realize that Existentialism hadn't amounted to much, had quickly been abandoned even by Sartre, who invented it (he became a Communist, then a Maoist). It was only a moment in a long argument in the West between the language of the gods and the language of a world without a supernatural life-support apparatus, a world without gods, a world of mere existence. This argument culminated first with Descartes' Radical Doubt and later, in the early twentieth century, in Edmund Husserl's *Cartesian Meditations*, after which philosophy veered sharply away from metaphysics into various branch lines: phenomenology, language philosophy, critical theory, structuralism, etc. Existentialism, an extreme twentieth-century application of systematic doubt, is a version of positivism with a concomitant impoverishment in the ethical and emotional sphere; the human aspect of language wilts.

But at first reading, the critical attitude, the defiant rejection of traditional values, melded seamlessly with my hormones and the biases of the hour: late 1960s counter-culture, Vietnam war protests, the Free Speech Movement, and nationalist revivals in both English Canada and Quebec. Like many people, I read *L'Étranger* through the *zeitgeist*. I had lost my sense of humour, and in my yearning for simple positions, it never occurred to me that a novel might be beautiful, funny, tragic, and mysterious all at once.

The version of the novel (originally published in 1942) I read most recently was Joseph Laredo's Penguin Books translation, published as The Outsider. It is a scant book, 109 pages long, divided into two parts; six chapters in the first part, five in the second. The point of view is first person, the voice of Meursault. The first half of the book follows Meursault from the announcement of his mother's death through the vigil and funeral, his love affair with Marie, and his entanglement with the pimp Raymond Sintes to the murder; the second half of the book takes place in prison: interrogation, trial, sentencing. At the end, Meursault is sleepless, waiting to be called to the guillotine. But he is strangely happy.

The plot has a noir torque insofar as Meursault can be said to be the victim of cynical manipulation, in part due to his own self-destructive inadvertence, that leads to the guillotine. Much has been made of the plot similarities between *L'Étranger* and James M. Cain's *The Postman Always Ring Twice*, but there were plenty of French hardboiled noir models already, Francis Carco, for example, and, of course, Georges Simenon. And other influences are apparent; Kafka, easily, and Hemingway, whom Camus acknowledged in a published interview.

The noir plot presents Meursault as a somewhat dim bulb, awkward in most social situations, who becomes enmeshed in a sordid conspiracy with his pimp neighbor, Raymond Sintes, who befriends him one evening, professes mate-ship, and then convinces him to write a letter to Sintes' estranged mistress so he can get her alone and slap her around (which he does, then Meursault covers for him with the police). This dubious alliance with Sintes is the fatal first step that leads inexorably down a death spiral of misogyny, racism, colonialism, and macho violence to the murder on the beach. The Arab Meursault kills is, in fact, the mistress's brother, who is somewhat understandably trying to get even for her mistreatment.

If Camus is slumming (or experimenting) in what he called "the technique of the American novel" (*Lyrical and Critical Essays*), his larger influences and his philosophical integrity are in the French classical tradition. The result is a terse, cleverly composed novel that proceeds in clear, distinct steps, beginning with the death of the mother, complete with gorgeous, emblematic, set-piece scenes and enchanting grace notes. I think here of the hilarious and horrifying march to the funeral: the sun, the unbearable African heat, and the aged fiancé lagging farther and farther behind only to catch up again and again because he knows shortcuts across loops in the road. Or the comic gem of a scene (puts you in mind of Samuel Beckett) when Marie asks Meursault to marry her:

> That evening, Marie came round for me and asked me if I wanted to marry her. I said I didn't mind and we could do [it] if she wanted to. She then wanted to know if I loved her. I replied as I had done once already, that it didn't mean anything but that I probably didn't. "Why marry me then?" she said. I explained to her that it really didn't matter and that if she wanted to, we could get married. Anyway, she was the one who was asking me and I was simply saying yes. She then remarked that marriage was a serious matter. I said, "No." She didn't say anything for a moment and looked at me in silence. Then she spoke. She wanted to know if I'd have accepted the same proposal if it had come from another woman, with whom I had a similar relationship. I said, "Naturally." She then said she wondered if she loved me and, well, I had no idea about that. After another moment's silence, she mumbled that I was peculiar.

Or the magnificently staged scene in the visiting room at the prison when Marie appears and the lovers shout across the room at each other over the hubbub of other prisoners and visitors (mostly Arabs). Even the shooting scene is wonderful, perhaps the most beautifully written and sensuous scene in the book, brilliant with the anvil heat, the flashbulb glare of the sun, the glittering sand, and the sea. (There is a sun and glare pattern throughout the book.)

For grace notes, I mean deft little motifs like Meursault's clerical colleague Emanuel, dimmer than Meursault, so much so that Meursault kindly goes to the movies with him so he can explain the plots. Or the little robot woman, busily marking her radio guide (she comes to the trial, too). Or the little inset story about the Czech man who goes away from his village and

that I was still happy." Thus, the novel follows what Northrop Frye described as the classic U-shaped structure of comedy, from happiness with Marie to unhappiness after Meursault shoots the Arab to happiness on death row—albeit with considerable irony.

There are elements of caricature in *L'Étranger*, a lightness too easily missed when you are eighteen and struggling with a book narrated by a man waiting to have his head cut off. The interrogation and trial scenes are comical, with echoes of Kafka. We find the prosecutor proclaiming, "Yes, the gentlemen of the jury will take note. And they will conclude that a stranger may offer a cup of coffee, but that the son must refuse it beside the body of the one who brought him into the world"; then, in the same scene, the defense lawyer loses his temper and announces, "Here we have the epitome of this trial. Everything is true yet nothing is true!"

Meursault will insist on saying things like (describing his conversation with the examining magistrate): "I thought it most convenient that the legal system should take care of such details [finding him a defense lawyer]. I told him so." And, "On my way out I was even going to shake his hand, but I remembered just in time that I'd killed a man." And, on the first day of his trial, "In fact, in a way it would be interesting to watch a trial. I had never had the chance to see one before. 'Yes,' the other policeman said, 'but it ends up being boring.'"

The examining magistrate and the chaplain care less about facts than about the state of Meursault's beliefs, and they take his resistance personally. This is from a scene with the examining magistrate:

> But he interrupted me and pleaded with me one last time, drawing himself up to his full height and asking me if I believed in God. I said no. He sat down indignantly. He

told me that it was impossible, that all men believed in God, even those who couldn't face up to Him. That was his belief, and if he should ever doubt it, his life would become meaningless. 'Do you want my life to be meaningless?' he cried.

The examining magistrate is waving his crucifix and shouting during this interchange. Meursault feels threatened but realizes that's ridiculous because "I was the criminal." This is funny, hyperbolic, and thematic; the clash of belief and non-belief, traditional Judaeo-Christian truth versus Absurd truth, like matter and anti-matter, in a nutshell, with Meursault playing a blinking, deadpan, Buster Keaton naif.

Meursault is, throughout, enigmatic, naive, and uncalculating, also a bit bone-headed, short-sighted, tacitly racist and self-regarding. Because he doesn't analyze situations, doesn't look ahead, and can't imagine what other people think or feel, he is often quite surprised by life. For example, he is astonished to find that, in her dying days, his mother had friends, even a boyfriend (he doesn't remember how old she is either). He has a difficult time imagining that other people have lives when he is not present. So we have this great comic interchange between Meursault and Marie; she's just asked him to marry her and then she has to leave.

> For a while neither of us said anything. I wanted her to stay with me though and I told her that we could have dinner together at Celeste's. She'd really have liked to but she was doing something. We were near my place and I said goodbye to her. She looked at me. "Don't you want to know what I'm doing?" I did want to know, but I hadn't thought of asking.

In his Afterword to the Penguin edition, Camus writes that Meursault has a passion for the truth. He doesn't tell lies. But of

course that's not precisely the case. The pimp Sintes inveigles
Meursault into composing that misleading letter for the pur-
pose of luring his mistress into an ambush. And then Meursault lies when he vouches for Sintes to the police. Like his pal
Emanuel, he cannot read his life for plot. He loves the sun, days
on the beach, swimming with Marie, but he is easily bored,
has few inner resources, and, most importantly, has a limited
ability to comprehend social situations. He is neither passion-
ate nor heroic in the common use of those words; rather he
resembles someone suffering from mild Asperger's Syndrome.

The mystery of the novel is how Camus intends his reader
to read Meursault. Why did Meursault shoot the Arab? (And
why did he shoot him five times?) Is he meant to be an absurd
hero? In which case, he would be an accidental, rather milque-
toast hero. How closely should we identify author and character? Where does the fault line of irony cut? And how, especially,
are we to read his closing *cri de coeur*, "I'd been right, I was still
right, I was always right," when what is right includes abetting
a pimp and murdering an Arab?

Two issues make *L'Étranger* a difficult read in this respect.
First of all, Camus deliberately obscures the point of view: by
this I mean he chose a limited narrative consciousness (limited
but first person, thus unreliable if not pathological—see above
re Asperger's Syndrome). On his own say-so, Camus borrowed
this point-of-view structure from the American novel, not
James M. Cain, but Hemingway. Let me quote at length:

> But the technique of the American novel seems to me to
> lead to a dead end. I used it in *The Stranger*, it is true. But this
> was because it suited my purpose, which was to describe a
> man with no apparent awareness of his existence. By gen-
> eralizing this particular technique, we would end up with
> a universe of automatons and instincts. It would be a con-

siderable impoverishment. That is why, although I appreciate the real value of the American novel, I would give
a hundred Hemingways for one Stendhal. (*Lyrical and
Critical Essays*)

This is a complex passage, but Camus mentions Hemingway and we know from other sources that he particularly had
in mind the novel *The Sun Also Rises*, and the technique he is
referring to is Hemingway's strategy of ellipsis, leaving things
out. The narrator of that novel, Jake Barnes, describes what
happens and reports what people say, but he never tells the
reader why he can't consummate his (unspoken) love nor is
he much good at analyzing situations or taking the measure
of people. Even in dialogue, the general trend is for characters
to avoid talking about what they are talking about.

I could mention any number of instances of this technique in Hemingway and his myriad epigones. It's a style
Hemingway developed out of Modernism, via Gertrude
Stein, a heavily stylized, self-conscious, telegraphic narrative
mode that sometimes comes across like a Grade 3 reader: "We
often talked about bulls and bullfighters. I had stopped at the
Montoya for several years. We never talked for very long at a
time." In many ways, the language imitates the modus operandi of film, which almost completely eliminates character
thought except for soliloquies and voice-overs. The upshot
of the elliptical style is a character who seems unaware of his
own motives, the larger meaning of his actions, and even his
own thoughts. This austerity can present as Existentialist, is
often mistaken as such, when, in fact, it is not. Existentialism
is a philosophical position achieved by logic; the American
style (Hemingway's version) is sentimental and self-pitying; it
evolved out of disappointed idealism.

Camus contrasts Hemingway with the classical French
novelist—Stendhal, in this case—who fills page after page
with character thought, analysis of situations and reactions,

choreographs the murder the same as the sun at the mother's funeral? Why does Salamano remark that Meursault's mother loved his dog? Why does Meursault think of his mother when he hears Salamano weeping in the next room? Why do the mother and daughter (in the inset Czech story) kill the father? Why is the climactic murder scene so gorgeously oneiric with its crescendo of heat and glare as Meursault approaches the spring (*la source* in French—my goodness, what gets lost in translation)? And why is the Arab waiting for Meursault at the source, dressed in a suit, brandishing a knife? All at once, the image seems charged with more meaning than it can bear, over-determined as Freud would say.

Derrida said he always saw *L'Étranger* as an Algerian novel, before all the absurdist claptrap got loaded onto the text. The suppressed plot of the novel is about an Arab whose sister is seduced into prostitution by a white man who lives off her earnings and beats her up. The brother protests, so the white man beats him up, too. The brother and his friends follow the white people to the beach and there's a fight. Naturally, the white men win; they are used to dealing with coloured people. Then, mysteriously, as if in a dream, the novel dream, Meursault and the Arab meet again at the spring (source). Never mind why Meursault is there (the sun made him do it). Why is the Arab there? Even more mysterious. Waiting to be killed.

THE ARSONIST'S REVENGE

DAVID HELWIG's novella *The Stand-In* came to hand first when I was asked to write a cover comment for the book, yea, these many years ago (2001, I think). I read it, was entranced and enchanted by its incendiary delights. It presents a man, a wounded lover, a long-suffering husband, a bird watcher, a university professor (that most careful and restrained of professions), *in extremis*, who explodes decorum, wreaks revenge (mayhem and insult), and becomes utterly and gloriously himself (apotheosis). This is what art is best at, giving us the moment we all wish for but can never achieve.

To somewhat embellish what I wrote at the time: *The Stand-In* is a comic gem, by turns mordant, witty, and wise. It's a delicious novella of friendship, marriage, infidelity, plagiarism, and sly revenge. But it's also a fascinating meditation on irony, biography, badminton, the great Canadian painter James Wilson Morrice, also Flemish painting, mirror imagery, Ernest Thompson Seton and animal painting (especially birds and horses), and the self. David Helwig is a master of thematic weaving. His timing is impeccable. One has the impression of a ferocious intelligence at play—the effect is gorgeous, seductive, compelling, and liberating.

The Stand-In isn't a long book, about eighty pyrotechnic pages after you subtract the blanks and section titles, separated into three chapters. It's a dramatic monologue, three lectures delivered extemporaneously by an unnamed retired humanities professor, a last minute replacement for the famous Denman Tarrington who has mysteriously succumbed the week before on the green-tiled floor of a hotel bathroom in New York. Our narrator has gone over the edge, abandoned circumspection and control; he has the podium, his ancient rival is dead (he and Tarrington were, for years, colleagues at the hosting institution), he will joyfully and maliciously set the record straight. Tarrington goes up in flames, demonstrated to be a plagiarist (he wrote his essays off the narrator's ideas), a wife beater, a compulsive and boastful seducer (the narrator's wife ended up running away with him), and a flawed badminton player.

The governing principle of composition is digression and recursion. One amongst the digressions that keep popping up is the story of the story, or the history of two mismatched academic couples whose marriages exploded "that summer," the one of crucial memory. Denman Tarrington (DT, aka Delirium Tremens) was married to a tall, slightly awkward woman named Madeleine; the narrator's wife was Anne, a quick, pink-skinned woman who kept her secrets and made a smashing doubles badminton partner (Anne and the narrator would invariably trounce the Tarringtons on the court).

Tarrington pilfered the narrator's ideas and wrote them into sensational essays that made him an academic career far beyond the local horizons. The last summer, the summer before Tarrington left for a big job in the States, he and the narrator met in Paris. Infidelities were revealed. On his return to Canada, the narrator finds his wife away on an extended trip (that she keeps extending, never to return);

questioned by Madeleine, he tells her the truth about her husband. Madeleine disappears; Anne goes off with Tarrington: and the narrator lives on in the old house by the salt marshes until retirement, when, finally he too leaves town.

Much is revealed, but Helwig seeds his story with more mysteries. Where did Madeleine go, carrying what secrets? Who has been phoning the narrator in the night all these years, never speaking. And, finally, what happened to Tarrington in that New York hotel bathroom? *The Stand-In* opens with a description of the death scene:

> A week ago he was found dead on a green tile floor in front of a mirror covered with steam in a hotel near Lincoln Centre. As a result of that—misadventure let us call it—your committee had to find a replacement...

The narrator keeps referencing this scene throughout. The words "green" and "mirror" create a network of association and repetition. One might almost say, with only slight hyperbole, that the entire text is an improvisation on these twenty-six words: *A week ago he was found dead on a green tile floor in front of a mirror covered with steam in a hotel near Lincoln Centre.* And how, the reader asks, does the narrator know that room so intimately, the green tiles and the mirror and the steam? The mind leaps to suspicions of foul play, especially as, throughout *The Stand-In,* the narrator insists on reminiscing about his recent trip to New York, as if to implicate himself in a crime no one knows has been committed.

> In New York recently, I stood in the Metropolitan Museum and looked at a remarkable horse painting by Rosa Bonheur...

When I was in New York, just before I left, I stopped at
the Metropolitan Museum, almost as if I knew I would be
called on to come here and speak to you.

The structure of *The Stand-In* is exuberantly meandering—
digressions and suspensions abound. The river Meander of
antiquity, mentioned in Ovid, is touched upon. Here is the
passage from the *Metamorphoses*, wherein the river is used
as a metaphor for the construction of the famous Cretan
labyrinth:

> Minos resolves to remove the disgrace from his abode,
> and to enclose it in a habitation of many divisions, and
> an abode full of mazes. Dædalus, a man very famed for
> his skill in architecture, plans the work, and confounds
> the marks of distinction, and leads the eyes into mazy
> wanderings, by the intricacy of its various passages. No
> otherwise than as the limpid Mæander sports in the
> Phrygian fields, and flows backwards and forwards with
> its varying course, and, meeting itself, beholds its waters
> that are to follow, and fatigues its wandering current,
> now pointing to its source, and now to the open sea. Just
> so, Dædalus fills innumerable paths with windings; and
> scarcely can he himself return to the entrance, so great
> are the intricacies of the place. (*Metamorphoses*, Vol. VIII,
> Fable II, Henry T. Riley's 1851 literal translation, courtesy
> of Project Gutenberg)

The Stand-In, yes, flows backward and forward and winds
about and dwells in little eddies, a bravura performance of
apparently effortless oratorical grace and inventiveness; the
only contemporary work I can think of that is like it is Gordon
Lish's *My Romance*, which also purports to be a rhetorical *jeu
d'esprit*, an improvised speech. And both texts owe a huge debt

to Laurence Sterne, whose novel *Tristram Shandy* is a Moby
Dick of digression, a monstrous and delightful extravaganza
based on not pursuing anything in the straight line. I give you
here Sterne's own famous digression on digressions:

> *For in this long digression which I was accidentally led
> into, as in all my digressions (one only excepted) there is
> a master-stroke of digressive skill, the merit of which has
> all along, I fear, been over-looked by my reader,—not for
> want of penetration in him,—but because 'tis an excellence
> seldom looked for, or expected indeed, in a digression;—
> and it is this: That tho' my digressions are all fair, as you
> observe,—and that I fly off from what I am about, as far,
> and as often too, as any writer in Great Britain; yet I con-
> stantly take care to order affairs so that my main business
> does not stand still in my absence.*

I was just going, for example, to have given you the
great out-lines of my uncle Toby's most whimsical character;—when my aunt Dinah and the coachman came
across us, and led us a vagary some millions of miles into
the very heart of the planetary system: Notwithstanding
all this, you perceive that the drawing of my uncle Toby's
character went on gently all the time;—not the great con-
tours of it,—that was impossible,—but some familiar
strokes and faint designations of it, were here and there
touch'd on, as we went along, so that you are much better
acquainted with my uncle Toby now than you was before.

By this contrivance the machinery of my work is of
a species by itself; two contrary motions are introduced
into it, and reconciled, which were thought to be at vari-
ance with each other. In a word, my work is digressive,
and it is progressive too,—and at the same time.

This, Sir, is a very different story from that of the
earth's moving round her axis, in her diurnal rotation,
with her progress in her elliptick orbit which brings

about the year, and constitutes that variety and vicis-
situde of seasons we enjoy;—though I own it suggested
the thought,—as I believe the greatest of our boasted
improvements and discoveries have come from such tri-
fling hints.

Digressions, incontestably, are the sunshine;—they
are the life, the soul of reading!—take them out of this
book, for instance,—you might as well take the book
along with them;—one cold eternal winter would reign
in every page of it; restore them to the writer;—he steps
forth like a bridegroom,—bids All-hail; brings in variety,
and forbids the appetite to fail.

All the dexterity is in the good cookery and manage-
ment of them, so as to be not only for the advantage of the
reader, but also of the author, whose distress, in this matter, is truly pitiable: For, if he begins a digression,—from
that moment, I observe, his whole work stands stock
still;—and if he goes on with his main work,—then there
is an end of his digression. (Laurence Sterne, *Tristram
Shandy*)

The digression is a beautiful thing, creates wheels within
wheels, elaborates (by interruption, suspense, conflict) in
the act of narration itself. An author's primary job is to create interest in the text (sentences, paragraphs, chapters, entire
works); he can tell an exciting story, but he can also tell an
exciting story in an exciting way (he can be less efficient in
the telling but perhaps more entertaining—even gain a secondary point thereby). Done correctly, the digression creates
surprise (where the hell is he going now?), suspense (when
is he going to get on with the story?), and a lovely sense of
relief (ah, we've come through, back to familiar ground). But
Helwig, a master of the form, doesn't do simple digressions.
He digresses within his digressions. And he has running

digressions (wherein he drops a digression, then returns to it, drops it and then returns—then he'll return to it or at least give nodding reference to it again much later in the text). The repetition of digression and reference end not in explosive chaos but in a pattern that sews the text together in a complex unity. It's an amazing act of literary prestidigitation.

I can only sketch in an example here, and taking it out of context grossly oversimplifies the textual play. The notional first lecture almost seems about to get under way when the narrator holds up a library discard copy of a biography of the painter James Wilson Morrice (text interspersed with slashing references to Denman Tarrington's habit of seducing students, possibly even encouraging success by spiking their drinks), but at once he sidetracks on the library stamps and invents (how would he know otherwise?) the story (biography) of a functionary employed at the Canadian Committee in Ottawa to choose and buy books to be distributed to Canadian military libraries to entertain and uplift service men and women. This functionary, a digression inside a digression, pops up again and again: he eventually leaves the Canadian Committee and works for the YMCA, he has a son, the son becomes an accountant who dabbles early in drugs, gets married, loses his wife, and ends up in New York for a job interview, occupying the room next door to Denman Tarrington, the night of his death. This young man, disturbed by the sound of running water, finally phones the hotel desk and thus prompts the discovery of the body, which leads to the narrator's invitation, etc. etc. The deft inventiveness and interweaving of this digressive tale, the little explosions of recognition along the way and at the end, are supernal delights. The title of the lecture series is "The Music of No Mind," and the structure is musical, like a fugue, compulsively recursive and repetitive.

But this sidetrack only lasts a couple of paragraphs before the narrator digresses on Somerset Maugham (odious man), who describes Morrice in a passage in his novel *The Moon and Sixpence*. The reader trusts there will be more on Maugham, and there is, but first Helwig chops back to biography and Denman Tarrington, his relations with a female colleague (in the audience at the lecture) and his habit of plagiarism and wife pilfering ("how his wife vanished, how my wife became his."). Then back via the colour green ("There was too the hint of green in the skin of the great DT as he lay dead on the floor of that New York hotel") to Morrice, who flooded his paintings with greens. But we only get started with this before the narrator is off on a discussion of the game of badminton, which they all seemed to play in those days. The narrator and his wife would play happy, netless games in the backyard overlooking the salt marshes, and of course the two couples wore on each other with epic doubles matches (with nets) ending invariably with Tarrington's rages when he lost.

I will stop there for you see how it goes. Helwig, in the guise of his racket-swinging, bird-counting narrator, is the most affable and graceful raconteur, the master of the amiable saber thrust through the heart—

> I do see Frank Puncheon and Annabelle Disney among you. Yes, Belle, I noticed your presence and those perfect new teeth. Did you notice mine? *Ou sont les dents d'antan?* You of course knew Denman when I did. I remember things he said about you, though I won't repeat them right now. We can meet later.

—who accompanies his coup-counting with casual (endless) erudition, a charming curiosity, and the capacity to bring everything back to the point, at least some point. ("To return: . . ."; "I was speaking about the colour green."; "Now in all this we have forgotten someone. We have forgotten that man in a small office in Ottawa. . .") You quickly get used to the program and trust the juggler, enjoy the comic timing, the sly juxtapositions and segues, always hungry for the next revelation or, better yet, the next nugget of syntactic invention.

The rumbustious eruption of digression has a tendency to become facile and frivolous unless tied to some essential ossature, unless the author as Sterne says, *"take care to order affairs so that my main business does not stand still in my absence."* Helwig takes care to counter the centripetal forces of his digressions, not just by continually returning to the story of the story (the history of the narrator, Anne, Tarrington, and Madeleine), but by deploying a vast repertoire of techniques. He does, first of all, yes, always return to the story, which advances methodically, if not chronologically, through the narrator's boyhood, wooing, and marriage, arrival at the campus ABD, the collegial years with much badminton playing and bird-watching, and finally the last summer, the trip to Paris, and the awful August explosion upon the narrator's return.

But Helwig does marvelous things otherwise to pull the reader in, to entertain. On one level (and with a writer of such striking panache and accomplishment it is always necessary to specify levels), he is also presenting a series of three lectures entitled "The Music of No Mind" (which always reminds me of the phrase "thought-tormented music" in Joyce's short story "The Dead"—I think they mutually explain one another). Apparently, the narrator had in mind a series of lectures on art, but he forgot his slides in a Montreal cab in his rush to catch his flight. The slides gone (and he keeps returning to this, too), he must actually describe the paintings. This is surely a knowing invention of Helwig's—ah, he'll lose the slides and then I can write some beautiful art descriptions. Deftly done. And what it means is that Helwig can, like the poet he is, pack his narrative with dramatic images, shadings, and sidelights offered by the paintings he describes.

The first lecture is notionally about the aforementioned J. W. Morrice, with digressions on the art of biography, on Somerset Maugham, Arnold Bennett, and Clive Bell (all of whom wrote about Morrice). The second lecture is notionally about the device of the convex mirror used over and over by fifteenth-century Flemish artists to ironize their paintings or show off their skills (all the paintings are of married or betrothed couples and mirrored images complicate their relationships; the narrator uses this section to talk, among other things, about his marriage). And the third lecture is about animal art, beginning with Ernest Thompson Seton (roped in ostensibly as a recurrence of the J. W. Morrice theme from the first chapter; Morrice knew Seton in Paris), thence to Audubon and the horses of Stubbs and Delacroix, and ending with a horse painting by Rosa Bonheur, which the narrator saw on his "recent" trip to New York. The art lectures are digressive (in keeping with the map of the whole), entertaining, and packed with nuggets of fascinating information about art and artists and the history of culture, not to mention the occasional brilliant *aperçu*—

> He [Morrice] drank, perhaps because the effect of alcohol was to make the sheen of the surfaces more intense; meaning and expectation gone, and what was left was pure notation, the love of paint. A kind of ontology, pure present. That's the reason music is only music in fragments, set free of time.

—not so much as to overburden the novella, and what is there is often linked by analogy or dramatic irony or some other form of patterning with the story of the story. For example, Ernest Thompson Seton, like the narrator, "struggled to be a devoted husband. That saddest of struggles."

And those convex mirrors often show a young couple, newlyweds or newly betrothed, but with another set of characters, spying, gossiping, or calculating just outside the main scene. (". . . and below all this, in the corner of the mirror, the head of the other woman.") Not only that but the narrator later recalls a visit to the local nursery with Anne and Madeleine. There is a spherical mirror hanging above, and the narrator momentarily catches Anne watching Madeleine who is watching him.

> Tarrington was absent. The three of us were about to go to her house for dinner, and the moment hovered over those three figures, caught in the shining globe. The mirror focused all these things to a point in my brain, and I half understood the meaning of it.

Again, I touch on moments to suggest modes of reading rather than make an attempt to be comprehensive. This text is dense and alive with patterning, cross-reference, echo, repetition, and shades.

Besides the lectures, the curious facts and meditations, and the various ironies and parallels (so that even when he is digressing, the narrator is talking about himself, the ineffable Denman Tarrington, and their wives), Helwig does an amazing amount of straight word patterning, flooding the zone, as it were, with particular words or ideas. And, as I say, these words are tied to the death scene, sketched at the opening of the first lecture: "It is death brought me here, ladies and gentleman." The narrator describes Tarrington's body stretched dead upon the green tiles before the steam-covered mirror of the New York hotel bathroom. And it turns out that Morrice used the colour green a lot in his paintings, such that the narrator calls him "the prince of greens," and thus we get passages of which this is only an example:

> I would not disparage the power of language, but have you ever tried to find words for colour, **green**, let us say?

We have that one word so we are driven to likenesses, metaphors. There are all the vegetable **greens**, the **green** of a stick of celery, the **green** of pepper squash, the **green**, not very different perhaps, of spinach, the **green** of the avocado, unknown in Canada in my youth but now so common, the **green** of unripe pears, unripe apples, leaves in bud and the mosses and fungi, all the **greens** of **green**. My daughter married a man named **Green**, and I have **Green** grandchildren. There was too the hint of **green** in the skin of the great DT as he lay dead on the floor of that New York hotel, blood no longer circulating, the skin first pale, then growing discoloured and under the fluorescent lights showing the slightest tendency to the pallor **verdurous**.

Then there are Morrice's **greens** and hints of **green**...

Green, fused with the death scene, with Tarrington's corpse, floods the first chapter/lecture but never completely disappears from the text, popping up now and then to remind us.

Similarly, the word "mirror" floods the zone of the second lecture. And again the reference to the death scene is made literal.

The **mirror** gives us an author's-eye-view of ourselves. When I walked into the bathroom, there was yet another, larger **mirror**, as there was in that hotel room in New York where Denman Tarrington could admire his naked body before stepping into the shower.

And we get whole pages of mirrors (you can make lovely zig-zag patterns with your pen if you follow them down the page). The aforementioned scene with the spherical mirror in the nursery actually appears in the third lecture, carrying the mirror pattern forward and tying the image not just to Tarrington's death but to the plot of the three survivors, the infidelities and betrayals of the narrator, Anne, and Madeleine.

Besides the word patterning, and there is more of that, of course, than I am giving you, Helwig, the author, in the guise of his alter ego, the narrator, is always busy making connections and reminding the reader, using techniques, again, that concentrate and focus the text. No word stands alone, without being connected to one or more other words; words and phrases have what we might call natural meaning in the narrative, in the sentence in which they occur, but the author is always adding a little something to make them vibrate in sympathy with other words or lines of thought, so that even in his most digressive digressions he is not off topic, merely expanding the meaning of the central idea.

On a very simple level, like any good orator, the narrator is always reminding the reader what has come before:

I said that I would return to the horses of Rosa Bonheur.

As I was telling you that story about Jim and the snowy owl...

When he introduced me two days ago, your president mentioned my little book...

You will of course remember from our first hour J. W. Morrice living on the Left Bank, painting and drinking.

He will also offer the occasional announcement of the plan by way of explicit foreshadowing; in the second lecture he says, apropos of birds: "Birds to come in my third lecture." And apropos of silence and crank phone calls: "I will have more to say about silence. The phone rings. No one there." This is bread-and-butter oratory, the practical stitching together of a lecture or a speech, the audience always needing to be reminded where it has been and where it is going, but this bread-and-butter technique is also a poetic contrivance that contributes focus and rhythm to any piece of prose. Like the audience patiently listening to the lecturer, the reader needs ever to be reminded where he is, where he has been, and where the text might lead.

Helwig also uses syntax and brute juxtaposition to connect motifs and story lines. For example, mirrors, badminton, and text structure (digression, in this case, and there is a running conceit that the structure of these three lectures is like a badminton match):

> We could, while on the subject of mirrors, take a step to
> one side and lob the bird ...

Or mirrors, badminton, and the narrator himself twinned, in imagination, with Tarrington:

> I reflected as I stood in the bathroom of that motel, that
> if he had survived to come here and speak, he would
> have looked **in the same mirror**, stood where I was now
> standing. The two of us were there for a moment, side by
> side, as though washing up after a brisk hour on the bad-
> minton court.

And here is a lovely juxtaposition, using anaphora to tie together story elements (Tarrington's corpse/the narrator standing next to Tarrington's wife that fateful August night when the comfortable veneer of their world went smash):

> **As easy to imagine** Tarrington's sturdy body lying dead
> in the steam. **As easy to imagine** Madeleine standing

beside me on the shore in the dark as the soft lap of the rising tide moved over our bare feet.

And sometimes a chance association is enough to allow the author to jam in a reference to another story line. For example, in discussing a painting by Memlinc, the narrator says:

> ... we are looking at a diptych, Virgin and Child in one wing, in the other the young donor, in his twenty-third year, it says. **Anne was in her twenty-third year when we married.** Where and how the two sections of the diptych were to be hung ...

Likewise, he will sometimes employ a simple time or place link to stitch together various story threads. In the following clever example, he begins with badminton, segues to Morrice (by time association), eight years old in Montreal, and thence to the narrator now (by place association):

> ... badminton, named, we are told, for the country estate of the duke of Beaufort where it is supposed to have originated in 1873. J. W. Morrice, our prince of all the greens, was then eight years old, a schoolboy in Montreal, attending school in a building which is now the site of the Ritz Carlton, where I eat from time to time.

Or sometimes Helwig will simply gather two story lines as a moment of pause before continuing, a reminder of the simultaneity of the multiple parallel lines of narrative, in this case, the lecture narrative and the memory of the past leading to Tarrington's death (and incidentally the subplot of the young accountant, son of the man in Ottawa, come to New York for a job interview).

I will gather my forces for a race to the end. Tarrington
lies in the steam **while** the man next door is picking up
the phone, **and we turn** to Quentin Matsys. Gold again
here...

Once again I can only hint at the riot of patterning and inter-
connectedness that Helwig presents to the reader. The text
becomes a shimmering surface of reflected lights, dazzling,
fizzy, and exciting. A confection, in a sense, and a brilliant
one.

Some of the confection, some of the patterning that holds
the text together, is purely rhetorical, existing as embellish-
ment, as in not communicating a message so much as con-
tributing energy and textual action (dramatic contrast and
tension, also rhythm). For example, there are amusing asides,
time stamps more than anything, rhythmic reminders: the
three men in the striped ties who attend the first lecture, then
disappear (one returns at the end of the third lecture)—amusing, meaningless, rhythmic. Likewise the narrator's insistent
reference to the three young, shaved women in the second
row (one disappears), the woman he overheard discussing
her tattoo in the library, and his ongoing asides to the college president. These bits of business with the audience form
a structural epanalepsis, a graceful book-end structure, the
shaved women and the striped ties occurring at the beginning
and at the end (the single striped tie appears in the last paragraph to signal the end of the last lecture).

Helwig also employs the rhetorical device of anadiplosis
throughout, nimble little connections between differently
purposed segments of text.

I recommend it [a W. Blair Bruce painting]. A sovereign
cure for melancholy, and a splendid spread of naked
belles.

Belles with an 'e'. An old-fashioned term, but appropriate to the period. Belle as in Annabelle, and you were, weren't you?

I was not always able to **read that face** [Anne's face].
   Difficult to **read the face** of Manet's woman, the one behind the bar ...

I don't possess Tarrington's gift of the apparently significant phrase, the grabby **oxymoron**.
   Moron and oxymoron. My brother was a moron—I know we don't use that word ...

I could go on, the word play is seemingly endless (despite the diminutive extent of the book). But I won't, just to leave room for a digression on Helwig's aphorisms. Aphorisms are brief symmetrical texts, usually constructed out of balanced antitheses. This against that. They often play with word meanings and slant juxtapositions in provocative ways. Helwig is a master of the form (there are innumerable variant subforms). And it is one of the delights of this book when he lets loose. Like all aphorisms, these sound witty and authoritative. I will quote a few, showing my habitual restraint but chafing under it.

... though we all know that while speech and truth may sleep in the same bed, they never marry.

Part of the genius of any artist is his blindness. What he cannot see makes possible what he can.

We can see the meaning of anything only when we are threatened with its loss.

The truth shall make you free, but the facts shall make you nervous.

Observation precedes taxonomy.

The last image of the image-laden text is the magnificent horse painting, *The Horse Fair*, by Rosa Bonheur in the Metropolitan Museum of Art. Rose Happiness, the narrator keeps reminding us. As he also keeps reminding us that he went to see the painting on his recent visit to New York.

I do not quite know what this horse image means but am not averse to a certain open-endedness in the texts I admire. *The Stand-In* is a rich and exciting read, a bravura performance of the art by a writer who is "on the page" in so many ways you care less about what he means than about enjoying the ride. I said at the beginning that the text is seeded with mysteries. How did Denman Tarrington die? Who is making those mysterious phone calls in the night? And what happened to Tarrington's wife Madeleine? *The Stand-In* is a mystery story, a story of mysteries. Those persistent phone calls, reminiscent of the subterranean sounds in Poe's "The Tell-Tale Heart," impel the reader to suspect that despite the scandalously confessional nature of the lectures, some secret gnaws at the narrator, a secret he will take to the grave, or at least past the last page of the book, which, yes, closes on the magnificent image of those ponderous draft horses.

The Stand-In gleams with paradox. A confessional that conceals secrets, a series of lectures—a nonfiction form half-way between an essay and a speech—that tell a story, a performance piece that is written down and meant to be read, *The Stand-In* portrays an unremarkable former professor of the middling sort turned anarchist, suddenly bent on rupturing the placid decorum (and denial) of the small university town, cradle of his youthful ambitions, jealousies, betrayals, infidelities, and defeats. The structure of the three lectures seems to enact this destructive energy, seems itself chaotic, jumbled, and inchoate. But the chaos is only apparent, and the structure of the lectures is complex, knowing, and skillful. Not chaos but a wild dance.

David Helwig's friend Tom Marshall at Queen's University once wrote an intriguing essay—"The Bourgeois and the Arsonist"—about the author's early poems just then beginning to come out in books. Marshall thinks of Helwig as a writer divided, a bourgeois and simultaneously an arsonist, a practitioner of the plain style as a sort of voodoo against the explosive and chaotic energies that prowl beneath the surface. He cites a poem called "Reflections" from *Figures in a Landscape*; every night, as the homeowner gets ready for sleep, an arsonist runs across the yard outside. The homeowner (the bourgeois) cannot tear himself away.

> At night before I pull down the blinds
> to shut myself in my warm house,
> I stand still at the front window
> and wait for him to come from the dark,
> and every night as I wait, he comes,
> the arsonist running across my lawn
> with silent flame all through his hair,
> a mouth ignited by crackling laughter,
> lips that speak only one word, and eyes,
> that flash awake like a struck match.
>
> Every night when I see him there
> I try to draw my eyes away,
> pull down the blind and shut him out,
> but every night I stand and stare
> and watch him singeing the neat grass
> on flaming feet that dance, that dance.

I don't know if Marshall's analysis of Helwig, the author, stands; I leave the psychology to others. But it's instructive to put this poem next to *The Stand-In* and reflect, because in the novella Helwig invents a bourgeois character who unleashes the unruly forces of anarchy and revenge, an act of sly rebellion after a life of small concessions and delayed gratification. "I am too old to postpone gratification," says the narrator, having earlier suggested that the chief difference between the bourgeois and the criminal mind is the ability to delay gratification. In *The Stand-In*, Helwig solves the poem's dilemma by the simple stroke of turning the bourgeois homeowner into the arsonist-lecturer, the transformation infusing his language with a savage joy. His story is about the universal drama of repression and the perennial wish for pay-back; it's about the scandal and joy of letting down your hair and shivering the humiliating myths and pieties of everyday life. But there's more: a delightful inversion has taken place. Not only does the bourgeois become the arsonist, but the reader exchanges places with the bourgeois, mesmerized by the flame-wreathed spectre dancing across the lawn, envious and exhilarated.

Yet, oddly enough, the lecturer's performance of revenge is elegant and superbly controlled, the frenzy of reflection more like possession by a muse than anarchy. The River Meander does not, in fact, meander at all. And the last paradox of *The Stand-In* is the paradox of the controlled chaos of art; the bourgeois becomes an arsonist, the two together forcing a beautiful pressure on the language without, yes, offering a decision between the forces.

THE EROTICS OF RESTRAINT, OR THE ANGEL IN THE NOVEL

JANE AUSTEN'S *MANSFIELD PARK*

She simply felt a powerful inner resistance to paying any price in foreign currency.
— Christa Wolf, *The Quest for Christa T.*

1. The Angel in the Novel

CALL THIS an act of piety and self-education. Academia has sacrificed entire forests on the altar of Jane Austen, and I am not likely to add one whit to the pile. But her novel *Mansfield Park* has been gnawing at me for two decades, ever since I taught it at Skidmore College to a class of privileged young people who might have walked out of its pages. (One vivacious co-ed wore platform shoes and glitter on her eyelids and regularly skipped sessions to attend a mysterious court case on Martha's Vineyard.) My copy is a palimpsest of notes, multicoloured highlights, underlining, and plastic flags.

It's been through a basement flood, and the rippled pages have sprung from the spine. I have a digital copy on my computer, equally marked up—testament to my obsession.

Mansfield Park is a brilliant book, a great book, breathtaking in its invention and orchestration. The British critic of the novel Q. D. Leavis called it "the first modern novel in England." Yet it is alien territory for the contemporary reader. Whereas we live in a culture of instant gratification and intimate sharing, Austen's best people find impulse and promiscuous self-expression dangerous if not pernicious. They strive to train their thoughts and emotions like garden plants; they value comfort over adventure; they practice self-command, as they call it, learn self-sacrifice and restraint. For us restraint is tantamount to repression. It has been over a century since Freud's talking cure leapt from the analyst's couch to the living rooms of the West; self-denial (good) has become simply denial (bad).

In this regard, *Mansfield Park* is perhaps the quintessential Austen novel and the least romantic romance ever written. The heroine, Fanny Price, wins the love of her life, her cousin Edmund Bertram (an Anglican clergyman), not by pursuing the object of her affection but *by default* after the love of *his* life, Mary Crawford, comes up morally short. It's not what Mary does that's wrong; it's the way she thinks. Mary Crawford calls her brother's adultery a "folly," while straight arrow Edmund calls it a "dreadful crime." Fanny Price, the last woman standing after the implosion of the Bertram and Crawford families, goes even further, calling it a "sin of the first magnitude," here touching the Christian bedrock that defines the moral structure of the book. Everything hangs on a fine discrimination of ethical intention, and Fanny is the only one who gets it right.

Fanny Price is a good person, a paragon—humble, grateful, dutiful, self-sacrificing, and restrained. She's very much like two other reticent, long-suffering Austen heroines, Elinor Dashwood in *Sense and Sensibility* and Anne Elliott in *Persua-*

sion, except that in *Mansfield Park* Austen takes an uncharacteristically sharp turn into the theological underpinnings of early nineteenth-century English morality. Without Austen actually mentioning it (there are no prayers, sermons, church-goings, or appeals to God), the question of holiness suffuses the book. It does this obliquely via the ordination theme. In a letter to her sister, Austen wrote, "—it [*Mansfield Park*] shall be a complete change of subject—Ordination," that is, taking holy orders, becoming an Anglican priest (though, of course, it is not the heroine but her love interest who is ordained). Holiness may perhaps not be the correct word, since Austen keeps a tight rein on her otherworldly intimations. Her strategy is apophatic; she is more intent on describing the here and now and, through Fanny, critiquing its ethical superficiality than talking about faith, grace, and other divine interventions. With typical Austenian irony, she leaves it to her villain, Henry Crawford, to recognize Fanny's figurative divinity:

> You have qualities which I had not before supposed to exist in such a degree in any human creature. You have **some touches of the angel in you beyond what—not merely beyond what one sees, because one never sees anything like it—but beyond what one fancies might be.**

By virtue of his role, a priest is a mediator, a link between the divine and the human. This is what Edmund Bertram is meant to become as the novel opens. Austen constructs *his* plot as a triad: Edmund pulled in two directions between Mary Crawford and Fanny Price. Though, of course, Fanny doesn't tell Edmund she's in love, nor does he recognize her as a love object until the very end of the novel. She is rather an expression of his best moral and spiritual inclinations, a model, reminder, and example. Mary Crawford represents the seduction of worldly pleasure; Fanny represents a narrowly ethical life, self-denying, dutiful, restrained, and devout; and the novel is Edmund's *Pilgrim's Progress*.

What Fanny possesses that the other characters do not is an inner guide ("We have all a better guide in ourselves, if we would attend to it"), a principle of discrimination, and self-discipline. There is a beautiful thematic passage near the end of the novel that makes the point. This is Sir Thomas Bertram meditating on the catastrophic choices his children have made and the defects of the education he has given them:

> ... he gradually grew to feel that it had not been the most direful mistake in his plan of education. Something must have been wanting within, or time would have worn away much of its ill effect. He feared that **principle, active principle, had been wanting; that they had never been properly taught to govern their inclinations and tempers by that sense of duty which can alone suffice.**

The phrase "active principle" is an Evangelical Anglican keyword. See for example William Wilberforce's 1797 book *A Practical View of the Prevailing Religious System of Professed Christians: In the Higher and Middle Classes in this Country, Contrasted with Real Christianity*:

> Religion ... may be considered as the implantation of a vigorous and **active principle**; it is seated in the heart, where its authority is recognised as supreme, whence by degrees it expels whatever is opposed to it, and where it gradually brings all the affections and desires under its complete control and regulation.

This sentence can stand as a rough guide to understanding Fanny Price's character and the structure of the novel. Fanny doesn't have a plot in the usual sense of that term. At critical moments, she steadfastly refuses to act. But she bears an active principle in her heart, and her constant struggle is to school her thoughts and emotions toward goodness in a tainted world. You might call this a plot by another name, a mysteriously a-typical plot-that-refuses-plot, and Austen uses it to draw a line between *Mansfield Park*'s real Christians (Fanny and, finally, Edmund) and professed Christians (everyone else).

Austen was not an Evangelical (she had a brother, Henry, who became an Evangelical clergyman after a failed career in banking). But it is in the nature of novel writing to exaggerate positions for dramatic contrast. Evangelicals, influenced by European Protestantism, stressed individual faith, humility, and the ultimate sinfulness of mankind; think of them as Anglican born-agains but professing a nuanced distinction, not rebellion. They were rather dour, proto-Victorians in our stereotyped understanding of the word.

Yet the Evangelical emphasis on the heart behind the act, the inner intention, fits very well with Austen's own emphasis on Fanny Price's interiority, her dramatic soliloquies, her refusal to act where she cannot find a principled path, and her disapproval of frivolous amateur theatricals (precursors of what come to be thought of as Victorian values). It helps Austen find a dramatic perspective within the novel from which to judge the ethical superficiality of people like the Crawfords. A basic distinction to keep in mind when reading the novel is between characters who act out of principle and characters who act because they want something, whether it be money, admiration, or love. Austen announces the mercenary spin of *Mansfield Park*'s presiding ideology in the precise calculations of the first two sentences:

> About thirty years ago Miss Maria Ward, of Huntingdon, with **only seven thousand pounds**, had the good luck to captivate Sir Thomas Bertram, of Mansfield Park, in the county of Northampton, and to be thereby raised to

3. What Happens

The edition I am using (Penguin Classics, 1996) runs to 390
pages, divided into three volumes (that function much like
acts in a play, with dramatic climaxes at the end of each) and
forty-eight chapters. Fanny Price is the daughter of an impe-
cunious, disabled lieutenant of Marines with a "superfluity of
children," living in the major naval town of Portsmouth. At
the opening of the novel, Fanny goes to live in Northampton
with the wealthy Bertrams (Lady Bertram is her mother's
sister). Inviting her is an act of familial charity on the part of
Sir Thomas Bertram, and Fanny is never allowed to integrate
fully into the Bertram brood for this reason. Sir Thomas has
two sons and two daughters, Tom, Edmund, Julia, and Maria.
Edmund is the earnest second son; since he can't inherit the
estate, he is bent on being ordained a clergyman with a living
somewhere nearby. He befriends Fanny, helps with her education, and she falls in love with him without quite admitting
it to herself and certainly not to Edmund or anyone else; she
knows her place. Edmund loves her in his own way (as a sister,
he keeps repeating), admiring her for their similarities: sense
of duty, kindness, delicacy, and bookishness.

A fast, entertaining, and wealthy brother-and-sister duo,
Henry and Mary Crawford, move into the neighbourhood.
Edmund fancies Mary, and a cat-and-mouse, book-length
courtship ensues; Fanny watches and suffers. Henry Crawford is a delicious flirt; he goes after Julia, then Maria (who is
already engaged). Sir Thomas has left for Antigua to fix something untoward with his plantation. In his absence, the young
people get up to mischief that climaxes in a series of intense
and inappropriate flirtations during rehearsals for a little
amateur theatrical production they intend to perform, these
illicit flirtations only brought to a thunderous and embarrass-
ing halt on Sir Thomas's return (a book burning ensues, the
play books).

The young crowd scatters. Tom goes off to drink and gamble, Julia to socialize with friends and hunt a husband, Maria to her new husband's estate and town house. With no one else around to distract him, Henry Crawford pays suit to Fanny; he actually comes to recognize and value her good qualities, and he has good qualities of his own despite his impulsiveness (the reader is quite attracted at first, all the while knowing that Austen has dark plans for him). Henry makes an awkward marriage proposal; Sir Thomas becomes involved in forwarding the match, but despite his best efforts he can't convince Fanny to say yes to Henry. She has two good reasons, neither of which she can speak: she doesn't trust Henry and she's in love with Edmund. Annoyed by her silence, which he interprets as stubborn irrationality (Henry is rich, after all), Sir Thomas sends Fanny back to her family in Portsmouth to think things over in penitential squalor. This plan seems tantalizing close to working. Fanny immediately misses the Bertrams and their estate, her health suffers, and Henry visits her, showing moral improvement and steadfastness of intention.

But then, back in the social jungle of London, the veneer of propriety comes unglued. Henry and Maria reanimate their affections and, horror of horrors, defy convention by running away together. Julia also elopes—with an acquaintance from those amateur theatricals. Tom falls ill from carousing and returns to Mansfield Park on death's door. Finally, Edmund uncovers Mary's ethical superficiality and breaks off his relationship with her. Fanny has long recognized Mary's failings, but she has kept her mouth shut as usual, suffering in silence. She returns to Mansfield Park to help look after the wounded family, especially Edmund, who eventually emerges from his disappointment and recognizes her not only as a figurative sister but as a potential marriage partner. They are set to live happily ever after. Not so poor Maria, who cannot be resuscitated from disgrace. She is packed off to a distant place, though still supported comfortably by those long-suffering and nameless slaves.

4. A Structure of Threes

The novel is elaborately and intricately orchestrated. This is its genius—a pure vein of what John Shade, the poet in Nabokov's *Pale Fire*, refers to as "combinatorial delight." You can't but admire that great rhythmic surges of action that intensify and climax at the end of each of the three volumes, the way each event neatly evolves out of previous events like segments of a telescope tube being pulled open, the gorgeously elaborated system of subplots, and the way every action, speech, and bit of stage property (Fanny's pony, the amber cross, Sir Thomas's bookcase, the fire in the East room) does double or triple duty as a symbol or parallel of something else. From my very first reading, I was fascinated by the Wilderness set piece at Rushworth's Sotherton estate, a gorgeously choreographed sequence of events that parallels and foreshadows the events of the entire novel. I can think of nothing as good save for the steeplechase chapter in *Anna Karenina* in which careless Vronsky rides his mare to death while Anna, with her husband in the stands, looks on.

You can imagine the various plots as a series of triangles (Austen seems to love triangles) with Henry-**Fanny**-Edmund at the centre (the refusal plot that magically turns into a marriage at the end): then Fanny-**Edmund**-Mary (Edmund torn between Mary and ordination), and Julia-**Henry**-Maria (flirtation and jealousy inspiring Maria's passion), which segues into Rushworth-**Maria**-Henry, which goes on hiatus while Henry chases Fanny—Fanny-**Henry**-Maria—only to explode in adulterous flames at the end. In effect, Austen sets Fanny's interior plot inside a system of multiple contrasting romantic subplots all on the restraint-lack of restraint (inaction-action) axis backed by her moral-religious thematics. All the subordinate plots involve various conventional erotic/romantic manoeuvres that seem shallow, venal, and inconstant in contrast with Fanny's persistent and unspoken love for Edmund. In other words, you learn to read the subplots from the critical point of view of the main plot and vice versa.

You can further imagine the book as a play in three acts, three large rhythmic units, huge waves that gather, surge, and break, and then begin again. Each of the three volumes ends with a climactic explosion that is followed in the beginning of the next volume with an aftermath (in the last volume, the aftermath is tacked on at the end): moral tidying up, expulsion or scattering of key characters, and a sense of gathering or redisposition of the dramatic forces. So Volume I looks at the intense flirtation amongst the young people climaxing in the rehearsals for the play and Sir Thomas's unexpected return. Volume II, after the tidying up, presents Sir Thomas's well-meant plan to launch Fanny socially in parallel with Henry Crawford's romantic pursuit (the one abetting and complicating the other), leading to his shocking marriage proposal and Fanny's even more shocking (to Sir Thomas) refusal.

Volume III begins with the tidying up, once again Sir Thomas trying to get control of events. This is not to be dismissed, though I use that phrase "tidying up," because the first scenes here between Fanny and Sir Thomas, Fanny and Henry, Fanny and Mary, and Fanny and Edmund are the absolute moral centre of the novel, stunningly well written and intense. This is where Fanny appears utterly exposed yet admirable. This is where you come to understand the net of crossed moral imperatives that enjoins her silence and the obdurate stubbornness of her essential soul. But then, yes, everyone scatters again, Fanny to Portsmouth, Henry to his estate, Mary to London, Edmund soon to follow, etc. Volume III ends dramatically with the offstage explosion of moral turpitude (Henry and Maria) in London and contains its own aftermath when Fanny and Edmund return to Mansfield Park. The narrator tells us what Sir Thomas has learned, brings Fanny and Edmund together, and then imagines their future bliss in the final chapter.

The two dramatic explosions at the ends of Volumes I and II both require Fanny to make difficult moral choices, difficult in that she is alone in her decision and everyone around her is against her, providing her with conventionally moral and prudential (venal) imperatives counter to her own. The theatrical rehearsals and Fanny's refusal to act a part in Volume I foreshadow Henry's marriage proposal and her refusal at the close of Volume II (and frame the inverse at the close of Volume III, when Mary Crawford fails to take a moral stand in regard to her brother's adultery). Both these climactic explosions involve disappointing Sir Thomas. At the beginning of Volume II (after the theatrical catastrophe), he is disappointed with everyone except Fanny and this is the beginning of his special attention to her that leads through her brother William's visit and the ball to Henry's proposal. But at the beginning of Volume III (after the proposal and refusal), Sir Thomas is disappointed with Fanny and no one else. This is a fascinating pattern of repetition and variation that foregrounds the special relationship of gratitude, duty, and regard that exists between Sir Thomas and Fanny. Sir Thomas is the source of all good things and her sense of gratitude towards him is such that at times of difficulty it renders her mute.

5. Absence at the Core

Naturally timid but also constrained by social inferiority and duty to her benefactors, the Bertram family, Fanny creates a strange and disturbing absence at the core of *Mansfield Park*. Instead of driving plot by acting to achieve her desires, Fanny Price spends most of her time observing the action of subordinate characters and struggling to achieve equanimity by restraining her feelings and constraining her thoughts. When Fanny does rouse herself to act, it is in the negative, a refusal to act (rather like Melville's Bartleby with his insistent "I would prefer not to"). As a result of her outward restraint, she is often misinterpreted, overlooked, and even forgotten by the other characters who *misread* her. In the novel's third volume, as I say, Austen exiles Fanny from the plot entirely, sending her to Portsmouth while the rest of the interested characters go to London (Fanny and the reader only know what happens via letters). There is a note of comedy in this; even the author, it seems, can dispense with Fanny's services.

It's a critical commonplace that Fanny is not universally admired among readers. C. S. Lewis called her out for insipidity.

> One of the most dangerous literary ventures is the little, shy, unimportant heroine whom none of the other characters value. The danger is that your readers may agree with the other characters. ("A Note on Jane Austen")

And an apoplectic Kingsley Amis (in a masterpiece of literary invective entitled "What Became of Jane Austen?") condemned Fanny as "a monster of complacency and pride who, under a cloak of cringing self-abasement, dominates and gives meaning to the novel." Such a reading, as Lewis suggested, is a consequence of the protagonist's passivity, which introduces a degree of what we might call hermeneutic play, a looseness of the novel joints. Without a concrete aim to define the meaning of a character's actions, readers may tilt to contrary interpretations. Yet it remains rather curious that Lewis, so religious himself, should miss the drama of Fanny Price's religiosity.

Conventional (I nearly typed *contemptible*) wisdom dictates that there can be no real story where the main character prefers to hide behind her needle work and is constantly being left out or behind while suffering without complaint. When writer-director Patricia Rozema made her 1999 movie, she felt compelled to tart up the novel with contemporary pastiche. She reinvented Fanny as a writer (like Jane Austen, using bits of Austen's own unpublished work), introduced a lesbian flirtation between Fanny and Mary Crawford, turned poor, dozy Lady Bertram into a drug addict, and forced Sir Thomas Bertram to renounce slavery. This is a travesty based on bad reading and the assumption (probably correct) that most contemporary readers are equally bad.

But it begs the question: How do you talk about absolute things in a novel? God, beauty, goodness, saints, and true love? Fanny's problem is how to be good (selfless, dutiful, principled, other-worldly) in a world in which all the usual assumptions swing towards calculation, mere prudence, or outright cupidity. The paradox of an absolutist morality is that there can be no acts of pure selflessness in the real world; thus Fanny cannot act—hence her curiously apophatic aura: her disapproval, her silence, her stubborn refusals. She defines herself by demonstrating what she cannot do. Silence for her has the clarity of resolution; rather than do wrong or complain of others (also wrong), she will be mute.

But the novel is a child of technology, offspring of writing, paper, and the book, with a materialist bias. In a novel, it's difficult to speak of absolutes. In 1868, just as he was beginning his novel *The Idiot* (another novel about a Christ-like character), Dostoevsky wrote to his niece describing the difficulty of what he was trying to accomplish:

> The main idea of the novel is to portray a positively beautiful person. There's nothing more difficult than that in the whole world, and especially now. All the writers, and not just ours, but even all the European ones, who ever undertook the depiction of a *positively* beautiful person, always had to pass. Because it's a measureless ideal.

6. Desire, Restraint, & the Invention of Consciousness

There *is* plenty of sexual energy in *Mansfield Park*. No one writes more astutely about raging hormones, flirtation, and the role of jealousy as an erotic accelerant than Jane Austen. The Wilderness set piece and the play rehearsals following it are little masterpieces of erotic psychology and narrative foreplay; and the climax (pun intended) of the novel is a volcanic eruption of illicit desire; though it is off stage and not named as such, the implication is that Henry Crawford and Maria Bertram simply ran off and jumped into bed. In contrast, Fanny's sexuality lurks solely in the intensity of her regard for Edmund, and she never acts on it (the idea of marrying Edmund never crosses her mind). In her thoughts she constantly tamps down jealousy and expectation. She knows it is wrong even to hope that Edmund might give up on Mary Crawford, so she coaches herself to forebear and find solace in helping others (again this can be comical since she mostly finds solace helping dozy Lady Bertram with her stitches).

One of the most curious and original inventions of the book is Austen's use of the technique of free indirect discourse *avant la lettre* or at least long before James Joyce and Virginia Woolf popularized it. Instead of a plot—everyone can have a plot—Fanny has a very modern self-consciousness and inner turmoil. Instead of a dramatic action, she has a dramatic mental and emotional life based on a constant triangular effort to adjust her inner state between what she wants, what the world offers her, and a principled goodness. Her renunciation of her own desires paradoxically results in a richer inner self.

Edmund has a plot, while Fanny doesn't, but by virtue of being the central point of view, Fanny's character is prioritized for the reader. She is what Nabokov calls the novel's "sifting agent." We observe Edmund's state of mind through Fanny's eyes. Fanny watches, with a distanced concern that seems almost divine, loving but unable to intervene (act).

Her inaction in the external world is a direct result of her continuous and intense struggle to give justice to other people and tame her weaker impulses (inaction is thematically linked with morality). When she is silent, it is because a principle prevents her from speaking. But she is thinking.

In the manner of much of her inventiveness, Austen here borrows from Shakespeare, in particular his soliloquies. She elevates thought to the level of dialogue and erases the critical distance between the narrator and the mind of the character. It is as if we overhear Fanny's actual thoughts or she is talking out loud to herself (in intense intimacy with the reader). Here is a typical passage from the first volume, Fanny trying to parse her feelings and obligations when everyone is urging her to take a part—that is, to act, to perform on stage—in the amateur theatrical:

> ... she had begun to feel undecided as to what she ought to do; and as she walked round the room her doubts were increasing. Was she right in refusing what was so warmly asked, so strongly wished for—what might be so essential to a scheme on which some of those to whom she owed the greatest complaisance had set their hearts? Was it not ill-nature, selfishness, and a fear of exposing herself? And would Edmund's judgment, would his persuasion of Sir Thomas's disapprobation of the whole, be enough to justify her in a determined denial in spite of all the rest? **It would be so horrible to her to act that she was inclined to suspect the truth and purity of her own scruples**; and as she looked around her, the claims of her cousins to being obliged were strengthened by the sight of present upon present that she had received from them. The table between the windows was covered with work-boxes and netting-boxes which had been given her at different times, principally by Tom; and she grew bewildered as to the amount of the debt which all these kind remembrances produced.

Fanny defines a moral problem and proceeds by a run of rhetorical questions to examine her soul, her motives, and the various ethical principles involved (duty and gratitude to Sir Thomas, gratitude to cousins). She even suspects the nature of her own vehemence in resisting the invitation to act. I emphasize the crucial sentence in which scruples prevent her from acting because that's the key to her character and the ethical structure of the novel.

And amusingly enough, Fanny's self-restraint does have a certain erotic appeal both for Henry Crawford and Edmund Bertram. In fact, Edmund seems to find this abasement one of the most attractive things about Fanny Price. (I wrote an earlier version of this essay under the title "Bondage Lit.") Witness the masochistic (delight and pain mixed) scene near the end of the novel when Fanny fights to suppress every resentful, jealous, loving bone in her body in order to make herself available to Edmund as a sympathetic interlocutor so that he can freely bemoan and anatomize his breakup with Mary Crawford:

> How Fanny listened, with what curiosity and concern, what **pain** and what **delight**, how the **agitation** of his voice was watched, and **how carefully her own eyes were fixed on any object but himself**, may be imagined.

By the end of the scene Fanny has accomplished what she set out to do, which is to win Edmund's trust, create an intimate bond in his mind, and become his necessary confidante. "Fanny's friendship was all that he had to cling to."

7. Religion, Education, & The Amber Cross

The novel focuses on a contrast between Fanny Price and everyone else (each character representing a degree of superficiality and calculation if not outright corruption—Edmund

Bertram being nearest Fanny in goodness and poor Henry Crawford, in a tie with Maria Bertram, being the most remote). Austen situates Fanny in a transitional axis between a Christianity of ardent, principled practice and a new faux Christianity that is more about appearances, just as she is situated in a structural triangle of her own between Edmund Bertram and Henry Crawford.

As I say, there are no church-goings, prayers, sermons, or direct appeals to God in *Mansfield Park*, but the thematic orchestration of the novel is such that religion forms a crucial part of the discourse of the characters. No one goes to church in the novel, but the chapel scene at Sotherton is a set-piece illustration of a religious culture in transition. Fanny is disappointed; the signs of awe and mystery are absent, and the chapel is no longer a locus of family and community worship as it once was. This is also the scene in which Mary Crawford discovers Edmund's intention to be ordained but not before she has dropped a joke about the conventional image of lazy, gluttonous priests. There are no sermons in the novel either, but in the second volume Edmund and Henry Crawford have a lively discussion about giving sermons; Henry would love to give sermons but just once in a while before large audiences and in London.

And there is an ostentatiously symbolic sequence of scenes involving the Henry-Fanny-Edmund triangle and an amber cross Fanny's brother has given her. She wants to wear it to the ball in her honour that leads into the climax of Volume II, but she lacks a chain from which to hang it. Henry makes an awkward gift of a chain through his sister Mary, but just a little later Edmund comes through with a beautiful gold chain of his own, which Fanny likes better because it's from him. But she's in a tizzy, torn between the conventional obligation of gratitude to Henry and Mary and her heart's delight in Edmund's gift. At the last moment, fate (the author) saves Fanny when it turns out Henry's chain is too large and Edmund's fits the cross perfectly.

Finally, an "education" theme runs through *Mansfield Park*; I have not space to explore it except to mention in passing how it inflects the novel's Evangelical torque. The Bertram children's indiscretions raise the question: how does one learn proper restraint? how does one acquire the necessary active principle? And the novel's answer is: a proper religious education. This is clear in the expanded version of the thematic passage I cited earlier in the essay, Sir Thomas meditating on his children's errant ways.

> . . . he gradually grew to feel that it had not been the most **direful mistake in his plan of education**. Something must have been wanting within, or time would have worn away much of its ill effect. He feared that **principle, active principle**, had been wanting; that they had never been **properly taught** to govern their inclinations and tempers by that sense of duty which can alone suffice. **They had been instructed theoretically in their religion, but never required to bring it into daily practice**.

Mary and Henry, too, have been ruined by bad parenting. Henry's behaviour toward women, according to Mary, is detestable because "the Admiral's **lessons** have quite spoiled him." "**The effect of education**," observes Fanny (a bit primly), when Edmund moans about Mary's improper conversation. In contrast, Fanny escapes the deleterious effects of Bertram household by virtue of being an impoverished outsider in the family circle. The chief part of her education comes from Edmund, who, like her, is cut out of the social sweepstakes because he is pre-destined for the priesthood. Once again, Austen gives Henry Crawford the role of recognizing Fanny's essentially religious nature (and the connection between manners, principle, and religion):

> ... her **manners were the mirror of her own modest and elegant mind**. Nor was this all. Henry Crawford had too much sense not to feel the worth of **good principles** in a wife, though he was too little accustomed to serious reflection to know them by their proper name; but when he talked of her having such a steadiness and regularity of conduct, such a high notion of honour, and such an observance of decorum as might warrant any man in the fullest dependence on her **faith** and integrity, he expressed what was inspired by the knowledge of her being **well principled and religious**.

8. Acting & the Inner Drama of Holiness

The novel's inner drama of holiness is enacted on two parallel tracks, one truly inward while the other is more conventionally expressed in external action. While Fanny struggles with herself, taming her resentments and schooling herself to humility and self-denial, Edmund pursues the reluctant Mary Crawford (she can't imagine becoming a country parson's wife), at war with himself over her alarming frivolousness. Fanny's big dramatic moments are negative and come when she finds herself under relentless pressure to act in ways she finds objectionable, and she refuses.

This is a complex and subtle figure; the structure of the novel—plotless pivot reflected against dramatic subplots—enacts the theme of the novel, which is ultimately the nature of goodness in a contingent universe. The thematic construction of Fanny's plot-that-refuses-plot turns on a triple pun, three senses of the verb "to act": to act as in a play, performing a role for an audience; to act in life so as to achieve an effect, manipulate, entertain, or impress; and to act as a moral agent with consciousness intention. For a professional actor to act in a play is innocuous, morally neutral (Edmund makes this point). But for a person to pose or dissimulate to achieve an effect can be morally suspect, or in Fanny's absolute terms, evil.

Austen is emphatic; Fanny announces her inability to act twice.

> "Me!" cried Fanny, sitting down again with a most frightened look. "Indeed you must excuse me. **I could not act anything if you were to give me the world. No, indeed, I cannot act.**"

> "It is not that I am afraid of learning by heart," said Fanny, shocked to find herself at that moment the only speaker in the room, and to feel that almost every eye was upon her; "but **I really cannot act.**"

Her constitution, incorporating that active principle, is such that she cannot pretend, in life or on the stage. She is incapable. In life, she must pursue the principled course, and when she can't (for lack of good options or because of conflicting moral imperatives), she falls silent. If pressed, she begs off.

Edmund at first declines to act a part in the play until steamrolled by fears for Mary Crawford's virtue, a dismal shock to Fanny's heroic opinion (note the lapse into free indirect discourse).

> To be acting! After all his objections—objections so just and so public! After all that she had heard him say, and seen him look, and known him to be feeling. Could it be possible? Edmund so inconsistent! Was he not deceiving himself? Was he not wrong? Alas! it was all Miss Crawford's doing. She had seen her influence in every speech,

and was miserable ... **he was to act, and he was driven to it by the force of selfish inclinations only. Edmund had descended from that moral elevation which he had maintained before.**

In contrast to both Fanny and Edmund, Henry Crawford is a theatrical enthusiast from the get-go, using every rehearsal to flirt outrageously with Maria Bertram. Acting is his habit of being. He acts for entertainment, for applause, for effect, and to persuade, not out of principle. Austen repeatedly demonstrates Henry's inability to be genuine by knowing slips that are her specialty. While visiting Fanny in Portsmouth, Henry makes a show of taking responsibility for his estate and tenants (which, until then, he has mostly ignored).

> This was aimed, and well aimed, at Fanny. It was pleasing to hear him speak so properly; here he had been acting as he ought to do. To be the friend of the poor and the oppressed! Nothing could be more grateful to her; and she was on the point of giving him an approving look, **when it was all frightened off by his adding a something too pointed of his hoping soon to have an assistant, a friend, a guide in every plan of utility or charity for Everingham: a somebody that would make Everingham and all about it a dearer object than it had ever been yet.**

He cannot resist revealing that he has an ulterior motive, that he is acting not out of duty but out of a desire to engage Fanny's affection. His intentions are toward an audience and not the counsel of his heart. "But such were his habits that he could do nothing without a mixture of evil."

Holiness is a word falling into disuse (as are churches and the clergy). Nor are we accustomed to the idea that our acts are moral acts (we are more apt to call them "political" in this age of political correctness) that require rigorous self-inquiry as to motives, feelings, duties, and justice. Popular therapeutic dogma enjoins us not to feel guilt but to turn our traumas into identity stories. We do not learn anymore to criticize and correct our emotions. And we are apt to miss the pun on the verb "to act" and the essentially apophatic nature of its structure. Fanny defines what is right and good by refusing to be calculating, self-regarding, ingratiating, manipulative, or even shrewd about her prospects. She refuses to act on terms that most of the people in the novel find perfectly normal. She'll risk poverty and obloquy rather than betray principle and the man she loves (even when his own enthusiasms lead him elsewhere). And her torment must remain internal, always unspoken, again for the sake of principle.

9. The Via Negativa of Fiction

Apophasis, or the ancient *via negativa*, assumes that God is outside creation, that He is literally no thing, concludes that He cannot be seen, described, or communicated with, and proceeds to define Him by negatives. Conversely, the only way to know God directly is to bracket out the "things" of this world. This is the path Fanny Price takes—poverty, humility, and exile—until Jane Austen rescues her at the very end of the novel.

I can think of two other fictional works that follow the same conceit: the aforementioned "Bartleby, the Scrivener: A Story of Wall-Street" by Herman Melville and *The Quest for Christa T.* by Christa Wolf. Bartleby hires on as a lawyer's copyist but refuses to do chores ancillary to copying. "I would prefer not" is his refrain. He takes up residence in the lawyer's office and refuses to leave when he's fired. The lawyer moves, but Bartleby remains. When he's evicted, he haunts the entry and stairwell. He's arrested, sent to the Tombs, refuses food arranged for him by his former employer, and dies. Bartleby will not even act to preserve his life. Subsequently, it turns out that he has worked as a clerk in the Dead Letter Office in Washington, the repository of dead hopes, affections, and prayers. Bartleby's pallid otherworldliness derives not from religious conviction but from his association with death, which has unfitted him for life, imbued him with a reluctance to act in the world of affairs, and consigned him to the tomb.

The Quest for Christa T. is a fictional memoir of a spirited German girl named Christa who grows up in the time of National Socialism then lives as an adult under Soviet Communism, two rigidly prescriptive ideologies. The word "quest" in the title is ironic; as Christa Wolf tells us in her essays "The Conditions of Narrative," she has set out to create a sort of anti-myth to answer all the male-dominated literary quests. Wolf's heroine Christa is energetic, charming, and well-intentioned, but her story is a baffling litany of failure, breakdown, and self-defeating impulses. Eventually, she marries and bears a child, only to throw away domestic security for an affair. And then she dies of cancer having accomplished pretty much nothing. Again, this is a plot-that-refuses-plot, although Christa seems to want to act, she mysteriously stymies herself every step of the way.

The key to understanding Christa's failure-to-thrive lies in a counter story told through the novel's word patterns. Christa's life is full of teachers, mentors, advisors, and interested friends who counsel her to seek health and success by curbing her lively and imaginative impulses. Toe the party line, they say, and by this they don't only mean the Communist Party doxa but also the calculation and prudence necessary to get on in any system.

> To survive . . . has always been man's goal and always will
> be. This means that at all times conformity is the means
> to survival: adaptation, conformity at any price.

Conformity, self-extinction, it turns out, is a price that Christa, like Fanny Price, can't pay; as the novel progresses, words like success, adaptation, conformity, calculation, and measuring acquire a sinister aura, and Christa's failures begin to look like assertions of a self under pressure from all sides to live the life of compromise. Her "neurotic" and stubborn resistance, her refusal to deal in "false currency," her kenotic dying to the world are paradoxically essential to the preservation of an awakened self. What does it mean to be alive? the novel asks. "And of *the attempt to be oneself?*"

10. *The Ambiguous Construction of a Self*

What is truly paradoxical in *Mansfield Park* is the way it reaches beyond its satire on the marriage customs of Regency England, beyond the conventions of the romantic comedy, and beyond even its theological torque to tell a very modern story about the construction of a self. Much like Wolf's Christa T., Fanny forges her self not in any positive way but in resisting the imperatives, the forms, imposed on her by her society and the gaze of the individuals around her. She is not simply a passive character, she is symbolic, fused with theme. I don't want to, I can't act, I won't do that—Fanny Price's refrain. She defines what action is by not acting, she defines morality by refusing to act.

The climax of Fanny's nonplot is the sequence of scenes after the ball when she steadfastly persists in refusing to marry Henry Crawford. The fact that she cannot tell anyone that she loves Edmund, least of all Edmund himself, who is obstinately smitten with Mary, makes her appear irrationally stubborn. She remains cagey about her distrust of Henry. She can't tell Sir Thomas about it at all; she confides in Mary (discreetly) and Edmund (explicitly), but Mary passes Henry's flirtations off as harmless, and Edmund, too, minimizes Henry's faults and suggests that time will prove his constancy (weasel words).

Above all, Fanny cannot escape their watchful, measuring eyes. Fanny is alternately stunned, hunted, bludgeoned, humoured, and sent into exile, but she remains true to her principles. She is the poor, underclass cousin who has never stood up for herself before; but in these chapters she asserts herself against every authority, including the wishes of the man she loves. She even makes a speech (unique for Fanny) in which she enunciates what might be called the novel's quintessential moral (in a novel full of moral discrimination).

> "I *should* have thought," said Fanny, after a pause of recollection and exertion, "**that every woman must have felt the possibility of a man's not being approved, not being loved by someone of her sex, at least, let him be ever so agreeable**. Let him have all the perfections in the world, I think it ought not to be set down as certain, that a man must be acceptable to every woman he may happen to like himself.

This speech reads like a feminist call to arms; those sentiments certainly existed. It asserts Fanny's right of self-determination, and in the context of the novel, this radical selfhood stands against the ubiquitous dogma of property, propriety, income, estates, inheritance, class, and rank. By extension, it claims for any individual the right of refusal in the face of what the world offers. The basis of self is apophatic: the ability to say, I am not that, and I am not that either. What the world offers is contingent, mired in circumstance, calculation, and history, rated by pre-existing discourses (habits, traditions, forms). The soul proceeds by denial. It's struggle is less a matter of knowing itself as essence than of knowing when it is not itself. Sorting and discarding the trivia of life is the existential duty of the modern.

That Fanny (and the novel) can't quite live up to this transcendent declaration is a sign of the tension that exists between Austen's inspiration, the time in which she wrote, and her preferred genre, the romantic comedy. Fanny must marry Edmund Bertram despite the fact that as Edmund himself concedes, she is "too good for him." Even the narrator is only dimly celebratory about the upshot.

> With so much true merit and true love, and no want of fortune and friends, **the happiness of the married cousins must appear as secure as earthly happiness can be.**

This passage is sometimes construed as Austen's ironic commentary on the romance genre or the institution of marriage. But we must wait another 150 years for a manifest critique of that ending in the form of John Fowles's novel *The French Lieutenant's Woman,* in which the author offers readers the possibility that the disgraced, impoverished, abandoned female lead might continue to exist on her own and even prosper. When her lover finally appears after a gap of years, she remains cool, aloof—inviolable; she has her own life and no need of rescuing by a man.

THE LITERATURE OF EXTINCTION

1. Nostalgia (the Death of God)

I N HIS ESSAY "The Depreciated Legacy of Cervantes," Milan Kundera offers a poignant confession of allegiance to an outmoded Humanism and an aesthetic of lightness and play, which at the outset of the Modern Era already suggested every human possibility except, perhaps, the possibility that we might cease to be. I say outmoded, but Kundera himself recognizes that the world he inhabits is alien to the human project. He calls it the time of terminal paradoxes, a time conditioned by the unifying, simplifying engines of mass media (which, in his mind, are against the complexity of novels). The era we are talking of contains the birth and death of the individual, the death of God, everything from Pico della Mirandola's "Oration on the Dignity of Man" to the smoking furnaces of Bergen-Belsen.

But first there is a bloom, a divine afflatus. Rabelais invents the proto-novel out of the Menippean satire (from the Latin *satura*, a stuffed sausage, or a hodge-podge), which we might think of as the earliest outbreak of experimental literature. Menippus's work is now lost but by repute was characterized by irony, quotation, hybrid form, parody, and bawdy humour. Shortly after Rabelais, Cervantes writes a novel about a man rendered insane by books. A decade later, in 1615, he publishes a sequel, in which the hero has to deal with characters who have read the first book. An imitator (what we might today call a troll) is wandering around Spain calling himself Don Quixote. This causes Don Quixote such anxiety that he begs the local mayor to certify his authenticity as the real Don Quixote. *Don Quixote* is about the anxiety of a character dimly aware that he is trapped inside a book. In other words, Cervantes is already conscious of the bookishness of books and the games that can be played with the words and artifice of verisimilitude.

A hundred and fifty years later, Laurence Sterne composes a novel without a plot but containing the famous blank page (for the reader to write upon), the black page, and a chapter with plot diagrams. After Menippus, Rabelais, Cervantes, and Sterne, there are no more techniques of experiment to be invented; they are only reinvented with different explanations. But the novel itself takes a detour into what Kundera calls the realistic imperative. Novelistic experiment resurfaces in central Europe with the advent of various modernisms (with Schlegel's German Romanticism in the background; hence Kundera's love of irony and complexity) in the work of Broch and Musil and later the Polish experimentalist Witold Gombrowicz (whose novel *Cosmos* subtly echoes *Don Quixote*; it's about a character trapped in an image pattern). Kundera has here grasped a thread of experiment, of playfulness, that is also against the decline of values, the loss of Being, and the entropic tendency of modernity, which seeks only homogeneity and profit. (Cervantes is brilliant on the cruel and air-headed free spirits of kleptocratic late capitalism *avant la lettre*.)

2. Cynicism (Lifting the Veil)

What we more commonly call experimental literature, what we might now, in the twenty-first century, call Establishment experimentalism, arises in the late nineteenth century (for art, with the Impressionists) and the early twentieth century (for literature, with the Surrealists). It evolves as an outsider (Salon des Refusés, 1863) critique of a basket of Renaissance and Enlightenment assumptions about truth, reason, language, self, and God. It lifts the veil (as in *The Wizard of Oz*) on the comforting and Philistine illusions of the modern Humanist project.

The work is difficult because it's new, but not so new that it can't be understood with the help of a little theory. Nietzsche and Darwin, of course. But Ferdinand de Saussure's analysis of the structure of the linguistic sign accelerates much avantgarde invention by separating the sign from the signified, gesture from meaning. Much twentieth-century experimental art is based on the inversion of sign/signified priority. The American experimental novelist John Hawkes puts it succinctly when he says that plot, character, setting, and theme (conventional devices promoting the illusion of verisimilitude) are the enemies of the novel, while repeated image and repeated event are the true essence of literary prose. If there is no signified (meaning), then pattern, brute sound (sound poetry), dream (Surrealism), and the accidental and the ready-made (Duchamp) become acceptable avenues of art.

The author ceases to exist conceptually. So does the reader. Words float. As reality comes into question, so does the illusion of reality, as in literary realism and the techniques of verisimilitude. The emperor has no clothes. The veil must be lifted. This is an oddly Platonic critique of literary arts. In the *Republic*, Plato argues against poets because their words might, through the action of the imagination, lead readers to think something is true that is not (Plato did not much trust the intelligence of the common person).

This austere modernity, modernity-from-the-outside, separates itself from the consumer art of the nineteenth and twentieth centuries and becomes a High Art and a minority art. This new Establishment experimental art reaches its apotheosis in 2011 when Kenny Goldsmith (a professional academician) reads Brooklyn radio traffic reports at the White House as poetry. Now, found poems and erasure poetry are all the craze at the creative writing programs. Oulipo is the new, cool (old) thing. The rebellion of the rejects that began as a flank attack on the school art of early bourgeois capitalism has been coopted by late capitalism minus the human element.

3. The Return of the Repressed, or the Aesthetics of Extinction

History is a tide of concurrent stories that break over the present like waves (some people still think they are living this history or that history, the discourses persist in a zombie state). The old styles of experiment all persist today in varying degrees of vitality. The new experimentalism, the newest loosely gathered basket of foundational concepts, foresees a moment when this will all be washed away with the extinction of the race (now imminent; some say it has already happened). The new aesthetics flow from this moment.

We see the world more clearly now (we think). It's very small, dirty, crowded with people, and heating up. The Anthropocene is the new name given to the period of time (roughly beginning with the Neolithic) human beings have had a significant impact on the environment. Now we know there is no free lunch, and the hubris of our assumption that the earth was an infinite, free resource specially catered for us by the gods is beginning to look like a monumental gaffe.

Nor are we essentially different from the other orders of being (say, trees, rocks, newts); consciousness may be a neural anomaly, or as the A.I. researchers like to say, an emergent property, that is, a side effect of our neural interaction with whatever we are interacting with (just as the colour of an object is not a property of the object but a side effect of the wavelengths of light interacting with eye neurons). Not a self, a soul, a ghost in the machine, but a whisp of smoke, dream-like and temporary.

The new aesthetics, like the old aesthetics, have something to do with what we think reality is and how we might represent that in art. And as the Spanish novelist Germán Sierra suggests (in a remarkable essay called "Deep Media Fiction"), a good deal of what seems new is repackaged nostalgia for the human; we invent zombie fiction and sci fi movies in which corpses or androids develop a soul, often better than the humans they deal with (we are saved, in a sense, by passing along our humanity). But if what is real is something like waves and particles interacting in peculiar ways and consciousness is a byproduct, if as the philosopher (of the post-Anthropocene) Claire Colebrook suggests, everything tends towards "indifference" (which I take to be undifferentiated, chaotic, unconscious Being), then any sort of writing must engage with its own impossibility.

Any traditional form only reproduces the Humanist myth; but a formless book risks failure (unreadability). Reading Sierra's essay, I am reminded of Heidegger's effort to invent a philosophical language to describe Being. Language itself is a construct of consciousness, which is an emergent property and not a thing. We are talking about using a figment squared to describe something we cannot know. And so the new experimental writing falls back on the age-old devices of allegory, constructed chaos, and suggestive reference.

The operative word here is "suggestive"; the new literature is suggestive of a reality that cannot be described or even approached. Echoing Heidegger's obscurity on the subject of Being, Sierra writes in his essay that the new literature attempts "to get different portions of reality to emit vibrations that might (or might not) have any observable effect." It borrows, as constructive analogies, words like the uncanny from Freud and schizophrenia and deterritorialization from

Deleuze and Guattari. It borrows from cybernetics and computer programming (an appropriation that lends an eery, inhuman tenor to the writing as well as a pseudo-scientific authority), and it borrows from pop culture, horror movies, and science fiction (Lovecraft is an avatar).

The spate of dystopian books and movies of the last couple of decades are forerunners, always projecting a survival of something recognizably human. But the new experimental literature is using a human artefact, language, to imagine the post-human *without survival*. I am speaking here of Ccru Writing, work out of and inspired by the fabled Cybernetic Culture Research Unit at the University of Warwick, most notably Reza Negarestani's 2008 novel *Cyclonopedia: Complicity with Anonymous Materials*, a horrific Pynchonesque extravaganza about oil, the War on Terror, terror, and archaeology. "The Middle East is a sentient entity—it is alive!"

Terror is the dominant tone of the post-human, of End Times. How could we expect the inhuman to be anything but inhuman? In America, Bret Easton Ellis's fingerprints are everywhere. I am thinking especially of the serial killer in Blake Butler's *300,000,000* (2014) or the cyber-rhapsody of rape in Jan Ramjerdi's *RE>LA>VIR* (2000). "We are connected now. Basically I rape her in the ass with the barrel of my gun, handle shoved up my own cunt so I can come too." All in the form of a computer print-out.

Call such books disturbances in a field. Beauty, after all, is only a comforting Humanist illusion. Every time there is a revolution in our concept of reality, there is a fresh outburst of experiment in the arts, fresh disturbances in the field. The newest experiments embrace the entropic tendency of late modernity; they seek to vibrate in sympathy with the fundamental indifference of things. The project is paradoxical (even comical), sending a message–THE END IS NEAR–while trying to engage an audience. There is no message and there is no audience–soon(ish).

CONSCIOUSNESS & MASTURBATION

WITOLD GOMBROWICZ'S ONANOMANIACAL NOVEL *COSMOS*

WITOLD GOMBROWICZ leans toward Surrealism, but then he is also steeped in the history of philosophy. His brain is marinated in modernity, the twentieth-century critiques of the Enlightenment, Husserl's Crisis in Philosophy, the loss of Being, and the turn toward Phenomenology and Existentialism. So there is a loony side to what he is doing that, at the same time, is very serious and sophisticated, profoundly conversant with tradition while attempting to stand outside tradition. He has that flickering quality I have described elsewhere; his text is continuously oscillating between assertion and ironic subversion.

In *Cosmos*—the title makes it obvious—Gombrowicz is satirizing the phenomenology of world creation, the mental process by which we construct a frame of meaning for ourselves. Not the world (whatever that is), *my* world. Both inside and outside the novel (that is, in so-called real life), the modus operandi of consciousness is comically super-rational and simultaneously self-defeating (Husserl demonstrated that reason was never going to get where it said it was going). You (a subject, a consciousness) begin to notice hints of repetition and pattern; you look for other instances of the pattern in the chaotic flux of sensation; and eventually you decide the pattern is real. This is the procedure of reason and science. But, of course, in *Cosmos*, what seems real to the narrator is in fact utterly contingent and often ridiculous or even murderous.

Form cannot enclose reality, but form always threatens to become reality. That is the antinomy of the novel: you can't fit the world into a book, and yet form (read: custom, tradition, ideology, inter-personal expectation, etc.) is always threatening to derail the life of the individual, that is, there is always someone or some thing trying to fit you into his book. *Cosmos* is, in part, a horror story in which the monstrous evil is a form (in this case, a literary device) that haunts the narrator and eventually takes over his life. Instead of Godzilla or the mad slasher moving ineluctably toward its victim, the villain of *Cosmos* is an image pattern.

There are two other forces working on the human mind besides reason. One is the dark and unknowable current of desire; the narrator, whose name is Witold, can't sleep with the girl he's attracted to so he suddenly and incomprehensibly kills her cat (it's a sick joke, right? he orgasmically strangles her pussy). The second force is the desire or gaze of the other. As soon as you enter a relationship (however trivial), you begin to bend yourself to fulfill, oppose, or circumvent the desire (expectation, form) of the other. Even if you resist, the purity of selfhood has been corrupted. So you construct another self in secret, the masturbatory self, the self who doesn't have to relate or unmask himself before the eyes of the other (but who is corrupt, seedy, infantile, trivial, and evasive in any case).

Out of this triangle of forces, Gombrowicz creates a truly awe-ful, hilarious novel. The narrator discovers patterns and deduces meaning; his own sexual violence betrays reason; he discovers that the secret life of the adult male patriarch is one of chronic secret masturbation (the creation of a private, obsessive cosmos).

Gombrowicz was born in Poland in 1904; his family had estates (as in land with peasants attached, income streams for which they didn't have to work); like Vladimir Nabokov in St. Petersburg, Gombrowicz was a member of the wealthy, east European elite, multilingual, well educated, sophisticated, with antennae tuned to the major currents of the age. He was taught at home by foreign tutors in the style of an earlier era. But he was also bisexual and talks of jolly, disreputable, unspeakable adventures in suburban back lanes, which perhaps early set him apart from the conventions of the time. This is in his memoir *A Kind of Testament* and, more delicately—those Retiro Park adventures—in his diaries; Gombrowicz is the rare writer who made a literary subject of himself, creating, aside from his fiction and plays, a parallel opus of self-commentary. As a young man, he published a book of precocious short stories (*Bacacay*), a novel (*Ferdydurke*), and a play that was not produced, but he remained somewhat on the periphery of Polish cultural life, defiantly not seated at the literary high table (he had an I'll-reject-them-before-they-reject-me attitude).

Just before the outbreak of the Second World War when he was thirty-five, he signed on for a free promotional ocean voyage to Argentina as a journalist, only to discover when he landed in Buenos Aires that his country no long existed. Instead of returning to England with the ship, he chose to stay in Argentina, where he lived mostly in poverty-stricken obscurity for the next twenty-three years.

Late in his short life, his work began to be published again in Europe, in Polish emigré journals, then in Poland itself and in translation. He suddenly had enough money to return to the Old World, spent most of the rest of his time in France, had the good sense to marry a French-Canadian woman, his companion of the last few years, and died of asthma (the family disease) and heart failure just before his sixty-fifth birthday. He was lucky enough, before he died, to have seen his work celebrated, his plays produced to wild acclaim, and the money flowing in. And near the end he finished *Cosmos*, his fourth novel, the subject of this essay.

Cosmos is a little novel, about 157 pages in my edition (the old Grove Press 1970 version, translated by Eric Mosbacher from the French; there is a more recent Yale University Press translation from the Polish, which is no doubt more correct, but one falls in love with the books one falls in love with, and the Mosbacher paperback was already strewn with my notes when the new translation came out). The novel's ten chapters comprise not so much a continuous plot structure but a diptych: the first four chapters follow one action, the middle two are transitional, though nonetheless crucial, and the last four follow another action with additional characters.

In the first four chapters, two student acquaintances, Witold, the first-person (retrospective) narrator, and Fuchs, both with reasons of their own for wanting to get out of Warsaw for a few days, wander on foot, looking for lodging in the countryside near Zakopane, a town in southern Poland at the base of the Tatra Mountains. In the woods next to the road they spot a strange sight, a dead sparrow hung from a branch with a bit of wire. Shortly after, they find a room in a nearby boarding house operated by the Wojtys family: Leo, a retired bank employee, his wife Kulka, a niece Katasia (with a scarred mouth) who works as a maid, their daughter Lena, and Lena's husband Louis (they are newlyweds), who works as an architect.

Witold instantly develops an illicit passion for Lena, whom he associates with the corruption embodied in Katasia's misshapen lips (though, in fact, she doesn't seem corrupt to the reader). At the same time, Fuchs and Witold together begin to track a series of faint if suggestive signs and repetitions (beginning with hanged sparrow) that include enigmatic shapes and stains in the ceiling, a piece of wood dangling from some string in the garden, and so on. They break into Kata-sia's room looking for clues (bringing a frog in a box, which they intend to use as an alibi if they are caught; part of a frog image pattern that originates because Witold thinks Katasia's lips look reptilian—they move from side to side instead of up and down); then Witold climbs a tree outside Lena's room and spies on her getting ready for bed (he watches her husband hand her a teapot, a hilarious, surreal/Freudian displacement of conjugal desire that unmans him); and, finally, in a fit of violent, motiveless passion, he strangles her cat and hangs its body from a hook in the garden.

The fifth chapter is aftermath. Fuchs plays detective; the entire cast of characters stands around the cat discussing pos-sible scenarios and perpetrators, then everyone adjourns to the dining room while Louis buries the cat. In the sixth chap-ter, Leo breaks the dead cat tension by suggesting an excur-sion to the mountains to visit a panoramic view he remembers fondly from the days of his youth. They travel in two open car-riages and, along the way, pick up a wandering priest and two more newlywed couples, Lola and Lolo and Tolo and Jadec-zka, friends of Lena.

The last four chapters follow various intertwined plots in a version of the forest/wilderness convention borrowed from Shakespeare (or any number of writers, for example Jane Aus-ten's *Mansfield Park*). Being out in the hills and woods lets loose all sorts of erotic and subversive hanky-panky. Wander-ing alone, Witold encounters Lena also alone; it is possible but unclear that she shares his passion; they stand next to each other not talking because Witold can't bring himself to act on his own erotic impulse, which has somehow turned insidi-ously corrupt inside him, like a ingrown nail; he can't love because he is disgusted with himself (after all, it kind of inhibits you if you've strangled the girl's cat and haven't told her).

He wanders on and finds Leo alone; they have a long, loopy conversation about the secret little (masturbatory) habits one develops in defiance of a world where everyone is watching everyone else (in Leo's case, his bank manager and his wife Kulka). Leo confesses that he brought everyone to this place, not for the view (night is falling anyway) but to celebrate the anniversary of the one supreme sexual encounter of his life, with a cook in the woods nearby when he was a young man. (In other words, he got a blow job at the foot of a rock thirty years ago, he's dreamed about it all his life, and now he's brought his entire family with their friends to relive the moment. This becomes the climactic scene of the novel.)

Elsewhere, Lola and Lolo dislike Jadesczka; they flirt with her cavalry officer husband Tolo; Fuchs spies Jadesczka pressing herself against Lolo in the dark; the priest fiddles suggestively with his fingers; at dinner, everyone gets lit and Witold witnesses the priest and Jadesczka vomiting off the balcony. Night has fallen. Witold staggers into the woods again and comes upon Louis's corpse hanging from a branch, an apparent suicide. In an act of hyper-erotic, if not to say homoerotic symbol-making, he sticks his finger in the corpse's mouth and decides to hang Lena. But first he comes upon the priest, pushes him roughly and sticks his finger in the priest's mouth. He catches up with Lena, Fuchs, and the newlyweds as they meander after Leo in the dark. At the supreme moment, everyone stands around, unable to see in the murk, while Leo apparently masturbates beneath a rock that may or may not be the spot where the cook gave him pleasure all those years before. Then it starts to rain, and we jump ahead to a paragraph of aftermath: Lena catches a cold, Witold goes home to his parents. The last line reads: "Today we had chicken and rice for lunch."

This is all dark, funny, and very strange, an absurd horror story and frustrated romance, something like *A Midsummer*

Night's Wet Dream Meets The Tell-Tale Heart; Gombrowicz is
ever the playwright and parodist; there are theatrical groups,
multiple off-stage sounds, set-piece scenes, dramatic mono-
logues, and seven ensemble dinner table conversations; in his
memoir *A Kind of Testament*, Gombrowicz calls it his darkest
work. Behind the cockamamie love plot, something dreadful
and ill-understood pursues the narrator with ineluctable logic;
and the thing that pursues him is a form. The novel's fantasti-
cally elaborated structure of repetition, leitmotif, cross-reference, thematic meditation, and memory rehearsal gradually
assumes the character of fate and drives the story willy-nilly
towards its conclusion. Pattern becomes reality. "Hanging and
I were one," thinks Witold at the chilling moment when he
accepts his role as Lena's hangman. The two halves of the novel
are thus symmetrical; at the end of the first half, Witold hangs
Lena metonymically in the form of her cat; at the end of the
second half, he sets out to hang her.

In a conventionally constructed novel, motive drives plot. In
Cosmos, there is a conventional plot of sorts, or a parody of
plot. This is what an author does when, like Gombrowicz, he
is a formalist committed to escaping and evading the confines
of form. The so-called conventional plot turns on Witold's
illicit and covert desire for Lena, the married daughter of
the household. This Witold-Lena plot begins in the opening
pages of the novel as the two students are being shown the
room they will live in.

> A ray of sunlight coming in through the blind illumi-
> nated a patch of floor, and a smell of ivy and the **buzzing**
> of an insect also came in from the outside. All the same
> there was a surprise, for one of the beds was occupied.
> A woman was lying on it, and I had the feeling there was
> something **abnormal** about the way she was doing so,

though I had no idea what it was, whether it was because
there was nothing on the bed but the mattress, or because
one of her legs was lying on the metal springs, as the
mattress had slipped a bit. At all events the combination
of **leg and metal springs struck me on that hot, buzzing
day**.

I give you the long passage because it bears the DNA or hall-
mark of the entire novel beginning with the use of epanaleptic
buzzing/buzzing to frame Witold's vision of erotic feminin-
ity, the woman he cannot have (Quixote's Dulcinea). The word
"buzzing," repeated throughout the novel, is a tag for chaos,
for the riot of raw sensory impression the world supplies.

Inside the chaos frame, Witold discovers the sign of eros
in the form of a rumpled girl, out of place, "abnormal," possibly asleep, or lost in revery, or, yes, masturbating (a major
motif as the text presses forward) on an unmade bed. The
juxtaposition of the comically disembodied leg and the metal
springs adds a kinky, sadomasochistic element to the tableau,
which strikes Witold though, of course, he cannot understand
why—it has touched him below the level of consciousness at
the centre of desire.

Or: Out of this rhetorical frame of chaotic sense data,
the object emerges; that is, the discovery of Lena is also the
epistemic moment, a moment of recognition (Plato, Kant).
Cosmos is full of such iconic tableaus, scenes dense with metaphor and analogy; Gombrowicz understands that all objects
are objects of desire, infused with eros at the moment of their
awakening; the epistemic moment parallels the moment of
sexual recognition; thus the dual desire structure of the novel:
Witold yearns for the impossible Lena at the same time as he
obsessively yearns to discern pattern and order in the buzzing chaos, both ventures sharing the eroticized nature of all
desire. And, of course, the violent, sadomasochistic aspects

reflect the intuition that all knowledge—read Foucault—is corrupt with power relations.

From this ur-moment, the plot develops with a certain whacky inevitability. Witold discovers Lena is married. He associates her beautiful lips with Katasia's deformed lips, can't get the whiff of corruption out of his head. He tries to flirt with her (he thinks she might be flirting with him) in the most hilarious and adolescent way (minute hand movements). He climbs a tree and spies on her getting ready for bed. He kills her cat. Then he continues the so-called flirtation (resting his hand on the dining table near hers and touching his spoon— she touches her spoon, setting him afire). Alone in the forest, finally, they stand speechless next to one another while Witold mutely thinks about why he can't say a word to her.

This is the climax of the love plot in *Cosmos,* the moment when Witold's festering obsession turns inward and annihilates itself; or at least annihilates its direct connection with an object (Lena). Witold's absolute inability to get outside his own mind condemns him to denial, displacement, and violence (or masturbation). Instead of screwing Lena, he strangles her cat. Shortly after the scene with Lena in the forest, Witold finds Lena's husband hanging from a tree and performs a symbolic sex act on him (sticking his finger in the corpse's mouth—believe me we have enough textual links throughout the novel to know that a finger is a penis for Gombrowicz in this book).

The plot is thus a classic love story with jokes, a parody of the Eros the Bittersweet motif of the ancients, a love that is never satisfied, a love sickness, as it were, and the jokes are sick (in the best sense), puerile, seedy, erotic, surreal (oblique), and Freudian (displacement and denial). Withal there is ever the shadow of Gombrowicz's indefinite sexuality hovering: Witold's self-disgust, which has no motive in the text, and his ultimate act of sex with the dead man, sex with Death.

At the same time, it is an allegorical reconstruction of the act of knowing (simultaneously, the impossibility of truly knowing anything), the human relation between consciousness and its object, the other, the truth, as it were, which relation is presented here as corrupt with all the complications of romantic love. Knowledge in this sense is a confection. Gombrowicz uses the word "constellation" throughout to represent this sort of knowledge; constellation as in a group of stars like the Great Bear. There is no Great Bear in the sky, simply a picked-out pattern of stars we have come to identify as the Great Bear. All knowledge partakes of the idea of constellation. It is artificial, our projection of form onto the random. "Constellation" and "buzzing" thus form a structural pair of contraries; order and chaos, in the abstract; Witold and Fuchs are always trying to discover order in the buzzing chaos, that is, establish facts, become conscious of things.

Gombrowicz hates form but loves form; he can't escape form because that would look mad (schizophrenic), and, besides, he also loves to play with form. So he parodies form, exaggerates it, and turns it upside down (formal inversion is a key structure of the avant-garde novel). He writes a horror story in which pattern (form) becomes the terrible enemy of the human hero. In a conventional novel, plot is the foreground, the spine of the text; and the tapestry-like arrangements of imagery, theme, repetition, and cross-reference form the textural density of the background. In *Cosmos*, Gombrowicz inverts structure, places imagery, repetition, and cross-reference in the foreground and diminishes the plot; in fact, the plot is a bit nonsensical in conventional terms, truncated, frustrated, and parodic. Gombrowicz deploys these common narrative structures in a style of hyperbolic excess. He multiplies techniques that are often thought of as ornamental— structures of elaboration such as image and word patterning, repetition, thematic forcing, analogy—then he turns the novel upside down (from its conventional orientation) and allows the ornaments to determine the characters' actions; the image pattern hijacks the plot.

In the sixth chapter, the travel chapter, the beginning of the excursion segment, Witold, at loose ends after killing the cat, wants the safety and predictability of form. What he actually says is that he wants a literary technique to which to submit himself, one of those 'be careful what you wish for' moments, if there ever was one.

> What was I looking for? What was I looking for? A basic theme, a *Leitmotiv*, an axis, something of which I could take firm hold and use as a basis for reconstructing my personality here?

In fact, the "Leitmotiv" plot, as we might call it, the hanging plot, or the horror plot, is already in progress when Witold announces his desire. It actually begins prior to the conventional love plot on the second page of the novel when Witold and Fuchs spot the dead sparrow in the woods beside the road. Again, the object emerges out of chaos, out of a phantasmagoria of woodsy impressions just as Lena appeared on the unmade bed.

> Yes, it was a **sparrow**. A **sparrow hanging** from a bit of wire. It had been **hanged**. Its little head was bent and its **mouth** wide open. It was **hanging** by a bit of wire attached to a branch of a tree.
>
> Extraordinary. A **hanged** bird. A **hanged sparrow**. This shrieking **eccentricity** indicated that a human hand had penetrated this fastness. Who on earth could have done such a thing, and why? I wondered, standing in the midst of the **chaos, this proliferating vegetation with its endless complications**, my head full of the rattle and

clatter of the night-long train journey, insufficient sleep, the air and the sun and the tramp through the heat with this man Fuchs, and Jesia and my mother, the row about the letter and my rudeness to the old man, and Julius, and also Fuch's troubles with his chief at the office (about which he had told me), and the bad road, and the rust and the lumps of earth and heels, trouser-legs, stones, and **all this vegetation**, all culminating like a crowd **genuflecting** before this **hanged sparrow**–reigning triumphant and **eccentric** over this outlandish spot.

I give you the complete passage because again the DNA of the entire novel is represented, the object appearing out of a screen of chaos. Lena was abnormal, the sparrow is eccentric—something unusual draws the attention of the conscious subject. But in this case we don't have a conventional object of desire; we have a bizarre image that comes from nowhere and goes nowhere yet is unsettling, curious, and iconic. It draws the mind but is baffling. When Fuchs and Witold discover that bit of wood against the garden wall, hanging by a string, Witold's obsessive mind goes into overdrive. He kills and hangs the cat. Then he returns to the woods and finds the sparrow again, considerably the worse for wear.

...I strolled in the direction of the **sparrow**, I was plagued by the disproportionate role it played in my mind. It remained perpetually on the sidelines and kept obtruding itself, though **it was impossible to connect it with anything**...What mattered was that **something was advancing steadily in the foreground, assuming greater and greater importance and more insistently obtruding itself**. It derived from the fact of the cat that I had not just strangled but **hanged**...I had of course **hanged** it for lack of anything else to do with it...Yes, yes, but the fact remained that I had done it and, though the deed was my own, **it associated itself with the hangings of the sparrow and the bit of wood.** Now, three **hangings** were different from two, **they amounted to something**.

It behooves the reader to notice especially here the repetition of the word "something" because the something is the pattern, inchoate and vague but also somehow crystallizing along the edges of the narrative, accreting force by number, repetition, and rhyme.

> . . . I saw this must lead straight back to the cat. **Yes, there it was, it came creeping up, it came quite close, I could feel it.** I could feel the buried, **strangled** cat, **hanged between the sparrow and the bit of wood**, all three motionless where we had left them and made significant by their very immobility. Oh, the persistent **horror** of it. The farther away you were the closer they came. The more insignificant and meaningless they were, the greater their power and oppressiveness. **What a diabolical noose I had put around my neck.**

The repetition of hanged objects is the inscrutable horror that haunts (I love this passage for its Poe-ish overtones) Witold and ultimately drives him to pursue Lena with the intention of hanging her. Three repetitions are something; four are definitive; when Louis hangs himself, the repetition becomes compulsion, it becomes real in the motives and actions of the narrator.

> This made four. The sparrow, the bit of wood, the cat, and now Louis. What consistency, what logic...

Not only is Witold mesmerized by the logic (of aesthetic form, the insidious insistence of rhyme), but he is equally driven to reconnect the hanging and the mouth patterns that started together in the first sparrow passage ("It had been **hanged**. Its little head was bent and its **mouth** wide open."). Witold's penultimate actions (finger in the mouth of the dead man and the priest) are at best obscurely motivated through the plot line (by the psychological mechanism of displacement) but are explicitly motivated by the aesthetic (structural) need to connect two image patterns.

> At the same time I felt a deep satisfaction that at last a link had been established between '**mouth**' and '**hanging**'. It was I who had done it. At last. I felt as if I had fulfilled my mission.

As soon as Witold expresses the thought, he follows it with a decision to extend the image pattern, the series of hangings.

> The sparrow.
> The bit of wood.
> The cat.
> Louis.
> And now I should have to hang Lena.

This is the moment when the image pattern takes over the plot, a delicious and knowing moment, a metafictional sleight-of-hand that exposes the underpinning (or underwear) of all novels, which, yes, are just patterns of words on the page, not real people with real emotions and histories. Or as Roland Barthes, in his famous essay on Balzac, wrote, "in narrative, however, the discourse, rather than the characters, determines the actions."

At this point, it is important to acknowledge the complexity of the representation that is *Cosmos*, a book, a world, a universe; Gombrowicz has created a mad, glistening structure that spins, levitates, and oscillates (flickers). On one level, and in discussing all great works it is necessary to specify levels, he is having fun, punning, telling jokes, and writing parodies of other forms (detective novels, thrillers, horror novels, and love stories) while at the same time orchestrating a riot of conventional techniques (word patterns, set pieces, memory rehearsal, rhetorical flourishes); he writes, yes, a formally knowing novel turned inside out. On another level, he is describing the phenomenology of cognition. On another level, he is describing the creation and deformation of the self in the inter-human, the zone of social interaction, self and other, the realm of social-psychology. And on yet another level, he is talking about the creation of a work of art. In effect, *Cosmos* contains a heirarchy or system of thematic story lines that function like subplots in a more conventional novel; their structures are parallel: the creation of a world, the creation of a self, and the creation of a novel are analogous activities. This is why the author can dance from one meaning field to another with such speed.

In his memoir *A Kind of Testament*, Gombrowicz says two crucial things about *Cosmos*. First of all, he talks about the contrary human desires to escape form and embrace form. On the one hand, we all suffer the social "deformation" of others, the continual corruption of self by forms imposed from the outside. The gaze of the other, so to speak, degrades the form of the self (whatever that is) and renders us infantile and secretive. Leo, under the watchful eye of his bank manager and his wife, retreats into a set of tiny, rebellious rituals and masturbation. On the other hand, like Witold in the novel, we are subject to what Gombrowicz calls the Formal Imperative, "our innate need to complete incomplete form."

> …man, in his deepest essence, possesses something which
> I would call 'the Formal Imperative'. Something which is,
> it seems to me, indispensable to any organic creation. For

instance, take our innate need to complete incomplete
Form; every Form that has been started requires a com-
plement. When I say A, something compels me to say B,
and so on. This need to develop and complete, because of
a certain logic inherent in Form, plays an important part
in my work. In *Cosmos* the story is made up of certain
Forms which start off as embryos, insinuate themselves
into the book, and gradually become increasingly distinct ... like the idea of hanging ... (*A Kind of Testament*)

This antinomy, this paradox, is the essence of Gombrowicz's thought. Everything he does flows from the fact that we
humans are not one thing or another but an uneasy (rhythmic) oscillation between two contradictory desires—for form
and against form. It also explains why it is impossible for him
to write a more or less traditional, naturalistic novel and why
he cleaves to irony with its peculiar strobe-like, flickering
quality. In composing this novel called *Cosmos*, he escapes the
novel.

Gombrowicz's second telling statement in *A Kind of Testament* reads: "*Cosmos* is a novel which creates itself as it is
written." Which is another way of acknowledging that in a
novel like *Cosmos* form creates the content, that is, the image
pattern (hanging1, hanging2, hanging3) creates a demand
for more hangings (hanging4 and the intended hanging5,
Lena's hanging). What are at first random, disconnected signs
become connected in the Witold's mind and then take over
his mind, eventuating in action that is mostly inexplicable in
psychological terms—metonymy becomes reality.

Conventional novels are written out of the assumptions
of our ordinary lives: people are individual selves who more
or less know who they are and can form thoughts and plans
and motivate themselves to act to accomplish some desire.
If twentieth-century philosophy has put these everyday
assumptions into doubt, if in philosophical terms reality is

other than it seems, what sort of novel might follow? In *Cosmos*, Gombrowicz's alter ego Witold juxtaposes the two sorts of reality, two sorts of logic, the aesthetic logic of form and the more mundane and (now we know) equally doubtful logic of motive and reason.

> This made four. The sparrow, the bit of wood, the cat, and now Louis. What consistency, what logic. . . But it was a clumsy sort of logic, a rather too personal and private logic of my own. . . There was another possibility, this one on the lines of ordinary logic. He might have been the victim of blackmail, someone might have been persecuting him . . .

For the everyday human construction of experience, Gombrowicz substitutes the mysterious and inhuman energy of form (which is why he calls it his darkest novel). Structural (aesthetic) repetition, in the course of the novel, takes on the attributes of Fate for the ancients; for what else is the curse upon the House of Atreus than a form passed ineluctably from one generation to the next?

Witold discovers himself trapped in a form (a series of images), tangled in the perverse logic of repetition, and develops a horror of repetition. *Cosmos*, as I have said, is a horror novel. Upon discovering the dead man hanging, Witold thinks: "My horror—for it was horror—derived from the repetition, for the sparrow had been hanging just like this among the trees." In this sense, all beautiful texts, insofar as they practice this kind of elaborated structure of repetition, are uncanny, horrifying; rhyme is mechanical and inhuman, structure destroys reason.

ACKNOWLEDGEMENTS

"The Style of Alice Munro" *The Cambridge Companion to Alice Munro*, David Staines, ed., Cambridge University Press, 2016.

"Building Sentences" originally appeared as a series of four columns in the *National Post*, September 9-12, 2013.

"Making Friends with a Stranger: Albert Camus' *L'Étranger*" *Canadian Notes & Queries*, No. 93, 2015.

"Consciousness and Masturbation: Witold Gombrowicz's Onanomaniacal Novel *Cosmos*" *3:AM Magazine*, August 2014.

"The Arsonist's Revenge" *Canadian Notes & Queries*, Issue No. 94, Winter 2016, and in *David Helwig: Essays on his Work*, Ingrid Ruthig, ed., Guernica Press, 2018.

"The Erotics of Restraint, or the Angel in the Novel: A Note on Jane Austen's *Mansfield Park*" *The Brooklyn Rail*, Spring 2017.

"The Literature of Extinction" *American Book Review*, Vol. 37, No. 5, July/August 2016.